Our Country Year

Geoffrey Eley

Our Country Year

An East Midlands month-by-month diary of countryside life

BBC RADIO LINCOLNSHIRE
in association with the
EAST MIDLANDS TOURIST BOARD
1983

By the same author

FARMS OF BRITAIN
(with Sir Harold Sanders, then Professor
of Agriculture in the University of Reading)

COUNTRYSIDE SECRETS

MONA, ENCHANTED ISLAND

THE RUINED MAID

101 WILD PLANTS FOR THE KITCHEN

WILD FRUITS AND NUTS

HOME POULTRY KEEPING

BIRMINGHAM HERITAGE
(with Lady Zuckerman)

First published by BBC Radio Lincolnshire, Lincoln,
in association with the
East Midlands Tourist Board

Text copyright © Geoffrey Eley 1983
Illustrations copyright © John Dillow 1983

Book design by Douglas Martin Associates
Illustrations by John Dillow
(excepting those on pps 9, 18, 25, 28, 43, 53, 60, 76,
85, 96, 109, 127, 130)
Cover photograph by Thomas Durrant, Barmt Green,
Worcestershire
Printed in Great Britain by AB Printers Ltd.,
33 Cannock Street, Leicester

All rights reserved. No part of this publication
may be reproduced, stored in a retrieval system, or
transmitted, in any form, or by any means, electronic,
mechanical, photocopying, recording or otherwise,
without the prior permission of BBC Radio
Lincolnshire.

ISBN 0 563 20258 0

Contents

Foreword
His Grace the Duke of Rutland CBE

Introduction
Lawrie Bloomfield
(Manager,
BBC Radio Lincolnshire)

March
When Spring comes 10
Early butterflies 12
The mad March Hare 14
Caution – Toads ahead 16
Forecasting Summer 17

April
The drowning Badger 21
Blossom time 22
Truth about the Fox 24
Seven Swans 25
Yellow foremost 26
Peggy Dishwasher 27

May
Bluebell magic 30
Hawthorn recipes 32
The May Queen 34
In the Cowslips 36
With jar and net 38
Dawn chorus 41

June
Bees in our bonnets 43
Month of Roses 47
Country scents 48
The coastline 49
Owl on the 'phone 51
Chalkland prize 52

July
Time for a rest 53
Cure for migraine 55
At the lakeside 57
Canal revival 59
Study in lilac 60
Travelling alone 62

August
Harvest begins 66
At Haddon Hall 69
A noble catch 70
Old Wives' tales 70
Month of the blues 72
All gathered in 73
Haunted cottage 74

September
Season of mists... 76
Butterfly colours 78
Vanishing countryside 79
The Large Blue 81
Purple hills 83
Willie o' Douglas Dale 85

October
Nature's New Year 87
The Goose Fair 89
Back to the sunshine 90
A breakfast treat 91
Where are the Otters? 92
Come into my parlour... 93
Woodland antics 94

November
Late departures 96
A Thing of Beauty... 97
Hedge trimmings 98
Not all Beatrix Potter 101
Winter visitors 103

December
Snow is beautiful 104
How to feed birds 106
Romany friends 107
Silent waters 109
Christmas lore 110

January
Long knowledge 113
A two-faced month 115
Fair Maids 116
Counting Magpies 118

February
The bush telegraph 120
Candlemas forecasts 121
Galanthophiles 122
Valentine thoughts 123
In the stockyard 124
Fairyland of lace 125

Terms for Groups of Wildlife 129
A Countryman's Calendar 130
From Grandma's Scrapbook 134
About the author 136

Foreword

His Grace the Duke of Rutland CBE

OUR COUNTRY YEAR is a most knowledgeable and charming book about the countryside. It shows that the author has a real and fundamental knowledge of his subject.

The idea of monthly chapters enables him to describe in detail the effect of the seasons on our national fauna and flora, of which between three and four hundred different species figure in Dr Eley's book, many of them at some length. This chapter arrangement may seem self-evident to the minority of our population who live in the rural areas, but it enables the town and city dweller to understand Nature's ever-changing effect on rural life.

The detailed accounts throughout the book of our natural history and ancient country folklore and customs create a most fascinating overall picture of our heritage, and helps to enrich our lives.

The natural environment of all industrialised nations in the modern world is in danger from pressures of population, the constant development of rural land, and from pollution of all kinds. The effect of modern agricultural techniques, necessary in order to feed our population, must be balanced against our desire to protect the beauty of our countryside and the existence of wildlife. The greater enjoyment by the public of our National Parks and their access to remote rural areas creates, in turn, further problems. The high density of population in England, particularly in the Midlands, means that the environment requires special protection.

I am grateful that the author has been able to draw some inspiration from his visits to my country Estates and that he shows such appreciation of their natural beauty. I am sure this book will give a great deal of pleasure to the many people who love and appreciate our rural way of life.

Belvoir Castle, 1983

Introduction

Lawrie Bloomfield
Manager, BBC Radio Lincolnshire

IT IS A GIFT given to very few people to paint a picture using only words. It means that for a few fleeting moments even the blind can see... can imagine their own pictures which, if blind from birth, must of necessity be illusions. They are no less precious for that.

For just a few minutes each Monday, Dr Geoffrey Eley, brings his gift of painting word-pictures to thousands of listeners to Radio Lincolnshire. His ability enables even the sighted to see because, to be honest, so many people, myself included, go through life not properly using the sense of sight that God has given us.

It was this breath of fresh countryside air which Geoffrey brought to our microphones that made me think that we should enjoy the delights of his writing at our finger tips at times other than those when we're hurrying to or from work, to or from school or are in the midst of proverbial never-ending women's work.

A book!

Yes, that was it. BBC Radio Lincolnshire, which I like to think has been responsible for many good and pleasant things in the life of this county, could do no better for its first publication than a collection of those delightful countryside scripts.

It has the feel of all that's good in life. So if you're feeling down, uptight, or even on top of the world, 'Our Country Year' should prove to be just what the doctor ordered. It is, moreover, a book which is in effect a seasonal guide on how to get the best out of living in, or visiting, the countryside.

Lincoln, 1983

George Borrow in his *Lavengro:*

There's night and day, brother, both sweet things; sun, moon and stars, brother, all sweet things; there's likewise a wind on the heath. Life is very sweet brother; who would wish to die?

A home-made painted greetings card from the author's Victorian family album. A further example appears on p.127.

March

When Spring comes

'THROUGH all the changing scenes of life' runs the first line of a much-loved eighteenth century hymn and as far as this thought applies to the English countryside I count myself highly fortunate to live on the edge of the attractive Vale of Belvoir and from there to look out upon the life of our national heritage, the countryside.

Material for my writing and broadcasting is mostly gathered from around a Victorian cottage straddling the borders of Lincolnshire and Leicestershire. But items for my notebook also come from others of the five counties of the East Midlands (as defined by the Tourist Board in association with whom this book is published). I can indeed walk into three of these counties from the cottage door. Across the meadows lies the Viking Way long distance footpath, linking Oakham in Rutland with the Humber Bridge, and which here follows the pre-historic Sewstern Lane, a route the Romans also used. Added to this on-the-spot storehouse of Nature is 32 miles of towpath beside the Nottingham to Grantham canal, opened to narrow boats in 1797 and now an undisturbed paradise for wild life.

This countryside diary, based on my week by week broadcasts from BBC Radio Lincolnshire, starts not on New Year's Day in January but on the first day of March - the month in which Spring officially begins and winter weather has but little time to run. March, the month when bird song ceases to be a mere 'whistling in the dark' and becomes full blooded; March, the month when mates are chosen and nesting starts; March, the month when Hares go 'mad' and early butterflies wriggle out of their drab pupal jackets and unfurl exquisitely coloured wings; March, the month to see the first lambs on the farms and to find the first yellow Celandines and Coltsfoot flowers signalling the coming of Spring towards the end of the month.

Countrymen call it the 'month of many weathers', and it is perhaps as well to remember that the weather men class March as one of the five winter months, starting from November. There is, however, some comfort in the fact that, compared with the previous winter months, March has a good deal more sunshine - about four hours a day, on average. Even so, March weather can quickly switch from spells of warmish sunshine to biting cold winds and wintry showers - indeed, as the old saying goes, 'March can come in like a lamb and go out like a lion'.

People with their noses to the ground know that one month, or even season, can merge imperceptibly into the next and at this time of year Nature seems to play stop-go tricks. Some plants will stand still in a cold spell, their development totally stopped until the sun shines again; other plants push on regardless - hardy favourites like the cheerful yellow Lesser Celandine, the sultry Red Dead Nettle, the peaceful Primrose and that endearing ragamuffin of waste land - the Coltsfoot which, in its hurry to please us, shows off its yellow flowers before making many leaves.

Botanists say that as many as fifty kinds of wild flowers can be found in March - well, maybe they can in the milder South Country, but not on the east side of England. Never mind, we can find quite a number including Wood Anemones, apart from those I have already mentioned. I have sometimes found Wood Anemones in the very first few days of March - looking so frail as to make me think the next high wind would blow their heads off. But somehow this, in fact, does not happen - the wise little Anemone simply hangs its head and leans with the wind, and perhaps that is why in Greek legend it was called the wind flower. Incidently, few of our wild flowers have so many picturesque-sounding local names: in Warwickshire they call it Granny's Nightcap; in Wiltshire, Lady's Petticoat; and you may have heard it called Snake Flower in Lincolnshire - a connotation oddly linked with Austrian folklore which had it that the Wood Anemone is the favourite flower of snakes!

The Blackthorn is beginning to come out in the hedges and the

Cuckoo-Pint, or Lords-and-Ladies, is popping up among dead leaves in the hedge-bottoms. I like this strange plant with its cowl-shaped green and purple hood enclosing a stem which bears both male and female flowers. Cuckoo-Pint has a peculiar smell and this, together with its bright colours, is Nature's way of attracting small flies into the hood of the flower where the flies become trapped in downward-pointing hairs until they have done their job as pollinators. And, like the Wood Anemone, the Cuckoo-Pint also has many attractive country names. Here in the Midlands it is often called 'Adam and Eve', and in the West Country it is 'Baby-in-the-Cradle'. Another very apt country name for Cuckoo-Pint is 'Parson-in-the-Pulpit' but perhaps oddest of all is one I heard when I lived in the Weald of Kent – 'Kitty Come Down the Lane, Jump Up and Kiss Me'. Pretty, yes – but beware: the juicy-looking scarlet berries which come in the summer are poisonous, fatally so for children.

Early Butterflies

AT THE END of the first week in March there is just a suggestion of green in the hedgerows here in the Vale of Belvoir. The Hawthorn is still bare but the stout, brown shoots of the Elder, are putting out tufts of leaves, and the Wild Roses are already well clothed with their delicate, but vivid, foliage.

When the sun is out, and you can feel a bit of warmth, you might be lucky enough to see a Brimstone butterfly awakened from hibernation. A lovely sight indeed, its sulphur yellow wings glistening as it goes on its very characteristic zigzag flight, every now and again settling on a grassy bank, with wings closed. The Brimstone is not the only butterfly about just now – others to watch out for after their winter hibernation are the Red Admiral, the Peacock and the Tortoiseshell... he is the chap who so often shows himself off in early Spring with his frantic fluttering on a window pane. These very early butterflies are not, of course, *newly hatched*. In fact, they left their chrysalis stage last autumn, quite late on, and after flying around for a day or two, went into a winter sleep – until a burst of sunshine brings them out.

Among these spectacular 'early risers' I was once, as early as 5th March, lucky enough during a burst of sunshine to see a Red Admiral stirring himself in a pile of dead leaves in the hollow of a Willow tree down by the River Devon which flows at the foot of the cottage orchard. Two days later I saw my first Ladybird and a Lacewing or two – those slender insects with large wings covered with a lacework of veins. They are slow, clumsy fliers but great friends of the farmer and gardener, eating literally hundreds of aphids each in a day.

Mention of the Willow tree reminds me that this about the time that many of our nineteen different sorts of Willows come into flower along the banks of rivers and streams, and on railway track-sides. I suppose the most obvious is the Pussy Willow. This bush, like the Poplar tree, bears male and female flowers on separate bushes and the very showy golden-yellow catkins, beloved by children, are the male flowers; the female catkins are silky and silver coloured.

The Willow of almost any damp piece of ground, river or no river, is the Common Sallow and even if its catkins are not quite as spectacular as those of the Pussy Willow they help to provide the church with 'palm' for Palm Sunday.

Two other Willows are well worth looking out for on your walks. The Purple Willow grows as a tall bush, usually only near fresh water, and has male catkins tipped with attractive purple scales. In contrast to this handsome high bush is the Creeping Willow – a tiny, compact shrub only about a foot high which you must have seen some time or another behind the sand dunes along our coast. Its fat catkins are a greenish-yellow colour.

Willow trees are pollinated by insects and are great favourites with queen Bumblebees who go to the Willow for an early and rich supply of pollen and nectar on which to build their colonies. Besides the bees you can often see the trees swarming with flies – rather elegant little creatures with dark spots to their wings and known by the odd scientific name of Sepsis. (It is easy enough to drive along country lanes glancing from the car to the hedgerow trees and finding nothing in particular to catch your eye. But this apparent monotony of dark branches against a dull grey sky is deceptive... just get out of the car and stretch your legs and you will find plenty to see.)

A close relative of the Willow is the Poplar, with its long dangling catkins and should you be lucky enough to come across the variety known as the Black Poplar I think you will agree that it is a very impressive sight with its dark red catkins. In Lincolnshire it is much scarcer than it used to be and here is the reason: in the last fifty or so years the only new Black Poplars to be planted were all male trees and this sexual discrimination was due to the fact that *female* Black Poplars produce huge quantities of fluffy seeds and these stuck to ripe strawberries on fruit farms, so making the fruit unfit for market.

Going back, if I may, to that bit of sunshine that stirred the odd hibernating butterfly, I had on that particular walk another reward (if that is the right word) while the sun shone for a little while. Crossing the lane from a bank alongside an old mineral railway line was an Adder, or Viper, the only poisonous snake of our countryside. The Adder's colour varies a lot; I have seen them a normal brownish-yellow but I have also seen a black one with vivid white markings (over fifty years ago now, but I have never forgotten it – as a naughty little boy I tried to drown one coloured like that). Anyway, now is the time male Adders come out of hibernation, before the females, and their job is to stake out territory for breeding later on – very occasionally I have seen a pair of male Adders rearing up and trying to push one another over for supremacy of land.

Dangerous though they can be, I assure that if you do not touch an Adder (or perhaps accidentally tread on one) then they will not bite you. You can be sure your snake is an Adder if it has a row of zig-zag markings all down its back and a clearly defined V-shaped mark on the centre of its head. So, if you come across a snake *without* any of these markings most probably it is a harmless Grass Snake.

Silly, I know, but I myself must admit to being none too keen on snakes – harmless or otherwise – and so I am rather impressed by those people who can handle them with apparent pleasure (my step-daughter once put several newly-born grass snakes in the pocket of her jeans, forgot to tell her mother about them, and they were next seen floating around in the washing machine!) Yet the same girl is terrified of a harmless little spider in the house. All very odd. Now, where Adders are concerned, I think it is best to have a close look around before you start picking Violets or Primroses just now on some grassy bank – the more so when such a spot is warmed up a bit after days of blustery winds.

The Mad March Hare

ANOTHER joyous sight in the countryside around this time of year is that of Hares performing their 'dances'. What we are pleased to call 'mad March Hares' are the menfolk of the species trying to impress the girls before mating. At such times you will find they are almost oblivious of danger, letting you walk up quite near as they bound about, kicking and standing on their hind legs to 'box' and 'dance' in the courtship ritual.

A Hare I once watched intrigued me with its curious antics... after it left its resting place in some long grass (a Hare's 'form' is the correct term) this Hare suddenly turned at right angles to the course it was on and then leapt about twelve metres or more to the top of a ridge of higher-ground. I can only assume the reason for such behaviour is to break the scent-trail, just as a Hare does when it so frequently doubles back on its tracks as it runs across the field. I have never seen it, but my farmer neighbour tells me the Hare is a good swimmer when needs be – apparently they will even take a good swim for extra food and have been known to cross a wide stretch of the River Trent to reach a field of carrots.

Hares are, however, declining in numbers and the main reasons are modern farming techniques which reduce the number of years fields are under grass compared with cereals; more predators such as the Fox, now on the increase; and cold, wet Springs (such as 1983) when fewer female

Hares become pregnant and also produce smaller and fewer litters.

When you do see a pair of Hares 'boxing' nothing seems to frighten them – not even when one approaches them with a gun. But then, when a young man's fancy turns to love, who cares? 'Faint heart never won fair lady' as my grandfather was so fond of saying. I was too young at the time to know what he was on about – but such seasonal thoughts bring to mind the following lines about March from a little book called *The Country Way of Love:*

> The North wind blows for energy,
> The East wind blows for temper,
> The West wind blows for friendship,
> And the soft South wind for love.

And on that tender note let me return to the birds and the bees...

As the days lengthen this month not only do my few domestic hens respond to more daylight by laying more eggs but one cannot help noticing the wild birds singing again. A Thrush has been entertaining us loud and clear from the top of the Plum tree near the cottage bathroom window, and both the Wren and the Robin are every morning angrily proclaiming their particular stretches of the Ivy-encrusted hedge. Soon, to this welcome resident orchestra, will be added the songs of the first Spring migrant birds to arrive – and one of my favourites is the Willow Warbler, inconspicuous greenish-yellow in colour but with an unforgetable song: a rippling warble of short, sweet and sometimes plaintive notes which reach a crescendo of sound and then end softly, softly.

To look at, the Willow Warbler and its relative the Chiff-Chaff are very similar, but the Chiff-Chaff's song is a mere repetition of 'chiff-chaff... chiff-chaff' (hence its name). Now that March is here we shall soon be hearing these songs again but, meanwhile, a Lesser Spotted Woodpecker has been making himself heard by drumming on a hollow branch of an Oak tree – and what a handsome bird he is in his black, white and red livery. Woodpeckers do have a voice but they obviously must find this drumming with their beaks a better way of advertising themselves over a wide area – and getting food at the same time. Neither is the Woodpecker the only bird we hear 'drumming' away: there is a wet field alongside the old Grantham canal much loved by Snipe who produce the drumming sound as they dive swiftly and obliquely from overhead.

By the middle of March the wild birds are busy courting and mating and, my word, how very lyrical they are about it all! Listening to a pair of Stock Doves in an Ash tree, just over in what we call 'the long meadow', it became obvious why we sometimes use the phrase 'billing and cooing'. My attention was first drawn to the Doves by a loud and continuous flapping noise. At first I thought it might have been a bird trapped somewhere nearby and trying hard to free itself. Then I looked up at the Ash tree and there, more or less at the tip of a slender branch, I saw the male and female Doves 'a-billing and a-cooing' in a most impressive courtship scene. The birds made the branch of the tree swing up and down, every now and again parting to fly away just a few feet and then returning to the tree with much flapping of wings. Countrymen say early mating by those birds means an early Spring. Well, I do not know about that... but there is plenty such folklore and odd sayings. For instance, bird migrations back to England for nesting are sometimes called their 'honeymoon trips'. Another saying is that the first bright days of Spring 'fill the birds' hearts with love and their beaks with straw'.

Caution – Toads Ahead

DURING the month, and when the weather is mild, do look out for Toads because, after their long winter sleep and at the very first sign of Spring, these fascinating amphibians emerge from their underground hideaways and head for water in which to breed.

Toads travel at night – so do watch out for them crossing roads – and, most remarkable, they always head for the very same pond in which they were born. So do Frogs, come to that, but in neither case do we know *how* they do it. Some naturalists think the Toads and Frogs have an in-built 'dampness detector' but I do not accept this because, surely, if it was a simple question of detecting the dampness of air around a pond then – being anxious to breed – they would settle for the first pond they come across. But the Toads and Frogs do not do this; they press on and on until they *do* find that pond of their birth! I think the most likely theory is that ponds, like rivers, all have their individual smell – partly due to different constituents in the water and hence different sorts of plant life growing in it. If I am right, then perhaps the Toads and Frogs are guided to their home ponds by an acute sense of smell.

What an original idea of a certain district council in Hampshire to have chosen as its official symbol a nice fat green Toad covered in warts - this in preference to yet another lion rampant or majestic stag on their coat of arms. The council's chosen variety of Toad is the Natterjack species which apparently lives thereabouts but is decidely scarce in most places - the Natterjack is smaller than an ordinary Toad and has bigger warts on his skin.

I know that high winds in March can be a bit tiresome but never forget that there is magic too this month - magic, for instance, in the way towards the end of the month the Blackthorn blossom suddenly appears in snowy profusion. One day these hedgerow bushes look so dull, their bark black, but walk past them the next day and it is as though they had been covered with confetti.

When these little white petals fall, dark green leaves rapidly expand to encompass tiny plum-like purple fruits which, although too bitter to eat even when they are ripe, make that delicious Sloe gin. These berries are the ancestors of all our mouth-watering plums of today.

Years ago in Norfolk it was the custom in Autumn to make a sort of English port-wine from the ripe Blackthorn fruit and one old country doctor claimed that the drink was what he called 'the sovereign remedy for fevers caused by the sinister mists of the Fens and marshes'. The old physician may well have been on the right track since we know that the high mineral content of Sloe berries makes them much more nutritious than cultivated Plums.

The Blackthorn is a most useful wild plant: apart from the berries, its leaves were used to make English tea at the time in our history when high import duties put tea outside the range of ordinary folk. Nowadays the leaves remain on the bushes to provide the chief diet for caterpillars of the Magpie moth and Brimstone butterfly.

Forecasting Summer

TECHNICALLY, the first day of Spring, on March the 21st, is called the Spring Equinox and it is a day when, all over the world, the length of day equals the length of night. But, science apart, the first day of Spring is linked with a remarkably accurate bit of old weather folklore which I hope you will put to the test yourself.

The theory is that if the winds around the time of the Spring Equinox are for the most part blowing from the north and east (or in between) then we are more than likely to have a good summer; but if the winds

Violet

are mainly from the south-west or westerly then countrymen say that summer will be a poor one for sunshine.

With Spring in the air what a delight it is to hear and see a Skylark singing away as it flies higher and ever higher. But then the thought occurs to me that there is hardly a month in the whole twelve when I have not watched a Skylark trilling its way up to what Shakespeare called 'the gates of Heaven'. They even do it long after dark – proving that the Nightingale is not the only bird to sing at night.

I never think of Skylarks without recalling a very young London evacuee boy we had staying with us during the war on a small farm I then had in North Essex. The boy was from Bethnal Green in East London and he had never been in the countryside – grass to him meant a London park. One day the lad gazed intently at a soaring Skylark and shouted to my wife...

> Look 'missus, just look at that 'ere sparrer;
> 'e can't get up and 'e can't get down, and
> ain't 'e just a-hollerin.

The poet Shelley put it rather differently when wrote in his *Ode to a Skylark:*

> Teach us, sprite or bird,
> What sweet thoughts are thine:
> I have never heard
> Praise of love or wine
> That panted forth a flood of rapture so divine.

By the end of March, and if you will look carefully enough, newly-born birds can be found in the hedgerows. This year, a few days before the 31st, I made a close inspection of the thorn hedges around the cottage, looking for the nests of two pairs of Blackbirds who had been singing their hearts out in some Plum trees along the drive. What I found was not only the Blackbirds' nests but also one of a Thrush in the same hedge, all these nests containing pink-fleshed and featherless babies.

In the country it never matters much if you do not find exactly what you set out to see – there is always something else to reward you, and so it was that day. High up in the old and very tall Pear tree in the orchard I spotted the nest of a Mistle Thrush or what I used, as a lad in Warwickshire, to call the Storm Cock. This is one of my favourite birds. I love the way he sings so early in the year however rough the weather (I have heard him when it has been snowing) and this, of course, is why he is called the Storm Cock. It is said that when you hear the curious *chur-ing* call of the Mistle Thrush in dry weather it means rain is near.

The name Mistle Thrush is short for Mistletoe Thrush owing to this bird's great liking for Mistletoe berries – but since these berries are none too plentiful it also enjoys berries on Holly, Ivy and Mountain Ash trees. More often than not you will find their nests in wide forks between tree branches, often with no attempt at concealment. The Mistle Thrush is shy of people, except when you approach its nest, but otherwise it is a bold bird, often attacking Magpies, Jays and other species bigger than itself and thus earning its other nickname of 'Butcher-of-the-Woods'. If you do not already know this bird on sight you can distinguish it from the Song Thrush by its greyish tint and jerky flight, with white tips to the tail feathers. And it is quite a big bird – about eleven inches long.

Finally, for this start-of-Spring month of March, a word about Herons. Near the lakes at Belvoir Castle is a heronry and this month the handsome-looking birds have that 'Spring in the air' feeling. On a recent visit I counted about eight or nine nesting pairs, in each case the grey male Heron standing guard on a tree branch close to the nest itself on which his wife sat upon the eggs. A grand sight, made all the better since the total number of birds in this heronry has increased quite a lot in the last two or three years – a welcome change from so many instances these days of particular species of wild life decreasing.

Generally speaking, the most likely place you will be able to see Herons is in the Fens and marshes. They often stand among the reeds on one leg, eyes half closed and head hunched between the shoulders. Then, suddenly, the Heron will pounce on a fish – hitting it hard with its pick-axe of a beak to kill it.

A relative of the Heron is the much rarer Bittern, again a bird of the wet lands. Drainage of the marshes led to the Bittern ceasing to breed by 1850 but by the turn of the century they had, most fortunately, become re-established on the Norfolk Broads and elsewhere in Eastern England. You can hardly mistake a Bittern if you should be lucky enough to see one – apart from its buff-coloured plumage and its booming call (rather like a fog-horn at sea), the Bittern when disturbed on the ground does a sort of 'freezing' act with its neck outstretched and bill pointing skywards.

In both 1982 and 1983 a Blackbird has nested in the choir stalls at St. Botolph's Church in Boston, Lincolnshire. Each time the choir sings the Blackbird chirps in. Perhaps the organist should try it with that well-known seasonal piece by Mendelssohn.

April

The drowning Badger

BEFORE describing what is going on in the countryside this month, I have to admit to having well and truly, on April the First, been made an April Fool – and that by some young country children. A Badger, they said, was struggling in the water of the canal lock just across the water meadows from the cottage and would I please stop whatever I was doing in the garden and rescue the drowning animal?

A likely story indeed! But I fell for it, not in any way registering in my mind that it was 'April Fool's Day, so I put on my fisherman's waterproof trousers and headed for the canal side. Sure enough there *was* a carcase in the water – but it was one of a small flock of brown Welsh hill-sheep kept by the landlord of the former narrowboat men's inn alongside the old canal wharf! The unfortunate sheep had been drowned days before and a sorry fleece-sodden sight it was. Imagine the enormous delight of the village children able to shout at me – 'April Fool!'

Back in the cottage, the episode started me off delving a bit into countryside beliefs on the origin of such pranks on April the First each year, generation after generation. I turned up several explanations – so 'pay your penny and take your choice'. One version has it that April the First was the final day of the eight-day festivities which marked the

Roman calendar's New Year when this began on March 25th. In support of this theory I found this condescending quote of 1766:

> It became a day of extraordinary mirth and festivity, especially among the lower sort who are apt to pervert, and make bad use of, institutions.

Another writer considered Noah was to blame for sending a Dove out of the ark before the flood waters had subsided on the first day of the month – and, according to this version of the April Fool custom, 'anyone who was liable to forget the incident was punished by being sent on a fruitless errand'. After my drowning Badger affair, I appreciate the point! But before we leave the matter, I rather like the North Country expression of being made 'an April Noddy'. It comes from the tropical bird – a species of Tern – called a Noddy, which earned a reputation among early mariners for being exceptionally stupid.

Blossom time

APRIL – and what a lovely and eventful month it is in the countryside, with new things to see every time you go out. In fact, the very name April comes from the Latin word for 'opening' and the first day of this month is given a traditional opening in many European countries. The blossoming of Spring is at hand. Primroses, Violets, Celandines and Wood Anemones are all out and I shall not have to wait long for two of my particular annual delights – the flowering of the Crab Apple and Wild Cherry trees.

I think the red-streaked Crab Apple flowers are the loveliest of all tree blossoms and, my word, how they attract the bees and other pollinating insects! When you keep bees, as my wife does, the location of their chosen flowers is of great concern both to the bees and to us. We are lucky at the Lincolnshire cottage because, apart from our own small orchard of Apples, Pears and Plums, there is a big Crab Apple tree in a field just opposite and thickets of Blackthorn all along the lane. It is the same story with certain of the farm crops – my wife is always delighted when she sees our neighbours drilling the yellow-flowered Oilseed Rape within easy flying distance from the hives; this means that the bees will work the crop for pollen and nectar, giving the farmer a bigger yield and us plenty of honey.

A word associated with this month is, of course, showers. Everyone knows the saying 'April showers bring forth May flowers' but one you may not know is 'When April blows his horn 'tis good for both hay and corn' (here the word 'horn' is a reference to thunder and the squally showers of this month). But despite April showers it would be wrong to regard April as a rainy month; records collected at Kew Conservatory from 1916 to 1950 showed April to be the fourth *driest* month of the year, equal with May. And I like the old German bit of wisdom which says 'Sweet April sometimes wears a white hat' (this of course, meaning snow).

Much to my delight, a pair of Wrens have, for several years running, nested in the thorn hedge on the lane-side of the cottage. All through the winter I see the Wrens hopping around some old tree stumps just across the lawn from the kitchen window and coming for food at the bird table. At this time of year, when the Wrens are busy raising a new family, I cannot resist a daily inspection at close quarters – but I once made the mistake of putting my hand into the nest to see how many eggs there were in it. After I had done so the Wrens promptly deserted the cosy, moss-lined nest; of course, I should have remembered some of the things 'old Velveteen' told me as a boy – he was the gamekeeper on an estate adjoining my aunt's farm at Stonebridge, Warwickshire (now the site of the National Exhibition Centre!)

Not only did the gamekeeper warn me of the readiness with which disturbed Wrens will desert their nest; he also explained why the male Wren is unique in the bird world for his custom of building his own nest, separate from the family home, specifically to lodge in by himself and thus get an uninterrupted night's rest (I imagine quite a number of fathers of very young children and babies would consider the boss Wren to be a very wise and cunning little chap!) But despite my gamekeeper friend, I personally have my doubts about this so-called 'cock's nest'. I think it is more likely to be a previous year's nest restored and renovated, rather than a newly-built job. But whatever the truth of the matter is, such a spare nest provides peace and shelter. Wrens certainly build nests in some strange places – this year Radio Lincolnshire was told of a Wren nesting in a pair of dungarees hanging on a washing line.

The tiny Wren has more local pet names than any bird I know. For instance, because of its very short tail its called a Cutty in the North, or a Stumpy Toddy in Cheshire. Then from its diminutive size we get names like a Tidley Wren in Essex, a Mummy Ruffin in parts of Lincolnshire, and a Tintie in Nottinghamshire.

Not surprisingly with such an engaging little bird as the Wren, there is a lot of folklore about them. What is called a Wren Hunt is one of the most elaborate folk rituals still surviving in Britain and parts of Europe. The affair takes place between Christmas and Epiphany on January 6th, but there is a curious reversal of the accepted order of things at that religious period. Often the Wren, although regarded as a sacred bird, is killed and much is made of the disparity in the size of the bird and the importance accorded to it. I know of a village near Toulon, in Southern

France, where four men pretend to labour under the weight of a slaughtered Wren carried between two wooden sticks; and in Devon two men play the same ridiculous part, plus singing a song about their burden!

Truth about the Fox

A COTTAGER'S PIG (a Large White called Siegfried), a small domestic poultry flock and half a dozen beehives (jointly occupied by English and Italian workers) are as much part and parcel of my home life-style as the birds and beasts of the hedgerows and woods.

Sad to say, a Fox recently worked his way by night into the poultry run in the orchard and left again after killing at least ten laying hens and leaving most of them with open, bloody throats and headless. Bad enough luck, to be sure, with any type of poultry – but much more of a loss since the birds were not run-of-the-mill modern hybrids but pedigree Rhode Island Reds (I have since re-stocked with pure Brown Leghorns, a breed rarely seen today but which has been kept in my family for over fifty years).

What a lot of mistaken ideas people have about Foxes. From suburbia they are seen as cuddly, intelligent animals rummaging about in dustbins for a meagre living. The hard facts of killed lambs and poultry are simply disbelieved by many townspeople; neither is it sufficiently realised that not only has the Fox been officially classed as a pest since the Agriculture Act of 1947 but our Fox population is now bigger than it has ever been.

Poultry losses apart, it is also with regret that I report the death this Spring of one of our resident garden Blackbirds. The bird was one of a pair that had visited the bird-table all through the winter and she had just finished nest building in the hedge when one of the farm cats caught her. I chased and swore at the cat and it dropped the bird from its mouth, but by then our Blackbird was already dead.

I stayed around the hedge for a while and saw the cock Blackbird fly up into one of the Silver Birch trees, mourning the loss of his partner. However, as I know from previous observation of such occurrences, the male Blackbird would not mourn for long – somehow or other he would find another wife and bring her to the same nesting territory even though it proved fatal to number one. Even more surprising is the fact that should number two, by some outside chance, also meet with an untimely end then the male Blackbird will have no scruples about bringing in a number three to take her chance in exactly the same place.

My observations again proved correct; within three days of murder by the cat the amourous Blackbird had installed a new wife.

This is the time of the year which spells danger to any potential Frog living as part of a clump of frog-spawn... garden ponds can get overcrowded with Frogs and the survival rate of unhatched Tadpoles becomes low. It this applies to your pond, do give some of the spawn away to friends; I used to love watching spawn turn into Tadpoles in a home aquarium (still do, to be honest, when I can find any to bring home – and that is not so easy these days when farm fertilisers have so heavily reduced the number of field ponds with Frogs in them). Incidentally, if you want any more information about garden pond frog-spawn then the British Herpetological Society will be glad to advise you. Just write to the Society, c/o the Zoological Society, Regent's Park, London NW1.

Seven Swans

IT WAS recently my pleasure to observe the impressive sight of no less than seven Swans flying in perfect V-formation over our cottage. I have never before seen so many on the wing together; even just a pair of Swans flapping their 6-foot wings overhead makes an exciting country sound, let alone fourteen such wings – imagine the enormous power of that lot! Where this bomber-like formation was heading I know not; I know only that what I call our resident pair of Swans again nested on the canal bank, this year joined by a pair of Canada Geese nesting not far away. I am glad that the Swans, who usually pair for life, are safe so far this year, since we do have occasions when brainless vandals destroy the eggs, sometimes even shooting at them with air-guns.

There are, of course, several different types of Swan, but the one most commonly seen – the Mute Swan – is Britain's only resident species. For centuries Mute Swans were known as 'Royal birds' because only the King (or those licensed by the Royal Swanherd) could keep them on country estates. And you may not know that the Swan is one of the world's heaviest flying birds: they weigh around 40 lbs (nearly three stone in human weight tables).

It will be some little while yet before we see the new-born cygnets on the canal since Swans' eggs take as long as 36 days to hatch, but when the baby birds do arrive it is a lovely sight to watch the careful way the mother tends them, frequently using her webbed feet to raise the fluffy cygnets on to her back for a ride down the canal... rather like those 'trips round the bay' for the children at the seaside! (*Seven more Swans:* see end of chapter.)

Another recent entry in my broadcasting diary concerns one of the most beautifully-marked of all our birds and one by no means often seen – the Golden Plover. The pity is that I did not see it flying or feeding – the bird had been shot in the southern part of Lincolnshire and is now being preserved as a stuffed specimen in a glass case. However, it is a fine looking bird with yellow flecked plumage and – who knows – there may be others in the district which will survive here although Golden Plovers usually prefer hills and moors.

Not many days after being shown the Golden Plover I was at the village inn when a lady opened the door to tell us there was a hawk outside. Nothing very unusual about that; probably a Kestrel, I thought, deciding to go outside and take a look. But imagine my surprise on seeing a young man sitting beside the canal with a very handsome large two-tone brown bird chained to his arm. I am not, as the phrase goes, 'in the falconry scene' but a variety of these birds are occasionally brought to Belvoir Castle for special displays and falconry events. Even so, this particular bird was one of a species I had not seen there – a North American Buzzard and, believe it or not, worth every penny of £450 according to its 21-year old owner.

The American Buzzard's scientific name is Buzzard *Borealis* and it has a red-coloured tail – the only part of this somewhat fierce looking falcon that its owner would let me touch (and that at my own risk, I may say). What, I asked, is the bird fed on? Day-old chicks, replied the owner. Fine, but where would he get them from I wondered? The answer was simple enough – the Buzzard's owner works at a chick rearing station and they do not want all the cockerels that are hatched. Very convenient!

Yellow foremost

PRIMROSES are much on my mind in mid-April, particularly after seeing some very big patches of them on a railway embankment approaching

York. Generally speaking, the Primrose, like the Cowslip, is now much less prevalent than it used to be, particularly near towns, and I suspect the reason is too many people digging up the roots for the garden. This would also explain why Primroses make such a spectacular show on railway embankments unreachable by the public, as approaching York. Where folk *can* get at them, Primroses are more picked than any other wild flower except the Bluebell and do not get the best of chances to seed themselves.

Has it ever occurred to you to wonder why most of our early Spring flowers are yellow – Primroses, Cowslips, Dandelions, Kingcups, Celandines and others are all yellow? The answer is that as yellow stands out more brightly against neutral or dark backgrounds, Nature uses this colour to attract pollinating insects to these Spring flowers (and come to that, Man has copied Nature's laws in various forms of safety clothing and traffic signs).

We all think of the Primrose as a yellow flower. So, generally, it is – but in South Wales there is a form with pink flowers, and yet another variety of the Primrose, called the Bird's Eye, has lilac-coloured flowers with a yellow centre – like the eye of a bird. It is, however, very rare and I have found it only once – and then in that paradise of wild flowers, Teesdale in Yorkshire.

Primroses also have their medical uses. In the New Forest woodmen used to make an ointment from Primrose leaves boiled in lard and this was used to treat cuts; I have also been told of an old May Day custom in Derbyshire when bunches of Primroses were laid on the floor of cowsheds 'to protect cattle against witches'.

Peggy Dishwasher

WAGTAILS are birds that fascinate me.

I love to watch these immaculate and happy little creatures trotting jauntily and oh so delicately across a wet piece of land, or on the garden lawn after a shower, looking for worms. I much like the way that every now and again Pied Wagtails break into a run and suddenly leap into the air as though about to turn a somersault. Exhibitionism, you might say? No, you would be quite wrong to think that; or even to think they are just simply jumping for joy. The truth is that the Wagtail's busy little actions are their method of obtaining a meal now that the warmer air of April is full of tiny insects.

But what about the Thrush? Yes, he too patters over the turf – but he does it for worms he hopes to lure to the surface, whereas the Wagtail wanders about with the sole intent of snapping up insects he disturbs as they fly upwards and away. That Wagtail's run and a leap does for him what tapping and poking about on the turf does for the Thrush.

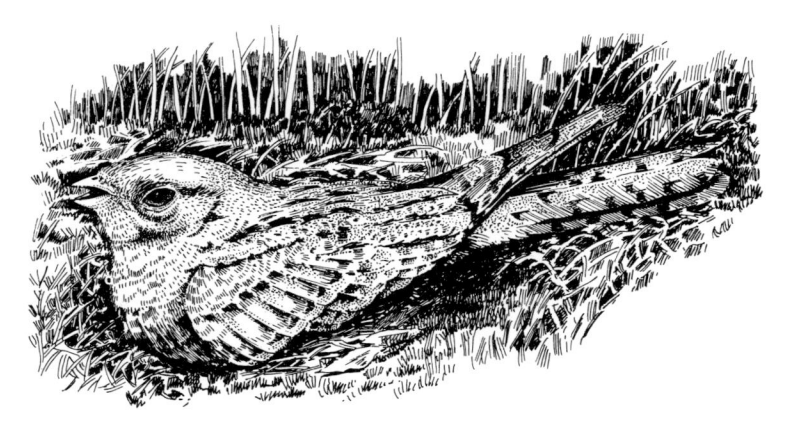

The name Wagtail is, of course, very apt. His tail wags up and down – almost as though it had a life of its own. Just watch this friendly, long-legged bird flashing about in the Spring sunshine then, quite abruptly, stopping and looking so perplexed – as one naturalist put it – 'like somebody trying to recall if he did, in fact, turn off the gas'.

No other bird on the wing looks so alarmed as does a Wagtail at finding itself in the air. And no other bird touches down with what looks like such a sigh of relief! This does not mean that a Wagtail is an unsure flyer – he can quite easily hover when seeking insects on the wing; he can also display his beauty looping about in the air.

I said the Wagtail is a friendly bird – so he is, even with other birds and animals with whom the Wagtail mixes in his gregarious manner. I see him on the farm running to greet the folded sheep; and I see him on the canal poking about in the weeds around the nests of Coot and Moorhen. If you get the chance, just watch a Wagtail treading water – a most attractive sight I assure you and no wonder the village children call her Peggy Dishwasher.

Coots, too, are worth pausing a while to watch. A group of these water birds can be one of the most placid sights in the countryside, yet, in a matter of moments, it can be a scene of great commotion. This happens if you move towards just one of the spaced-out group of birds – all the rest of them for some reason I do not understand start scurrying about and making a great deal of noise flapping their wings on the surface of the water. The same noisy display takes place should a bird of prey – say, for instance, the familiar Kestrel – come on the scene; and all this is such a great contrast to the normal tranquility of a gathering of Coot on lake or canal.

About thirty different species of migrant birds arrive this month, including the Chiff-Chaff, Willow Warbler, House Martin, Whitethroat, Swallow, Swift and – of course – the Cuckoo; and they get here in that order, so do keep a lively eye open for the Chiff-Chaff first. And, by the way, countrymen believe that it is a good sign when Swallows and House Martins build nests around or on your house and bad luck, therefore, to destroy such nests. Anyway, why on earth would anyone want to do such a horrid thing – to me, baby Swallows bobbing about on the clothes line ready for some flying practice is a sight to gladden the heart.

Spiders are another thing you should never harm. I know some people are ridiculously scared of Spiders, but I do not understand why. Spiders are both useful and most friendly little creatures of which, believe it or not, there are over five-hundred different species in this country alone. An old rhyme has it that:

If you wish to live and thrive
Let a spider run alive.

Be that true or false, I have certainly never, never killed a Spider. After all, you never know your luck and those little 'Money Spiders' are supposed to bring good fortune! Try examining a Spider sometime and you will see what a handsome creature he is. Attached to its thorax by a very small 'waist', the Spider's abdomen is beautifully figured with mosaic-like markings in the form of a cross.

The word Spider comes from 'spinder' – a spinner – and as a home builder the Spider certainly surpasses every other insect. Before winter he prepares a silken cell in which to keep warm, and a fine work of art it is. No wonder the Spider is referred to in the Book of Proverbs as 'One of the four things that are little upon the earth but exceedingly wise'. This is indeed true, and I might add that Spiders are exceedingly ingenious and persevering. Their beautiful webs are proof of ingenuity; their untiring energy, traditionally regarded as a prime example of perseverance. I shall have more to say about Spiders when we get to the autumn months when their webs hang so delicately on the hedges and garden gates.

Seven more Swans: I have collected the following classic literary references to Swans. Can you identify them?

1	The Sweet Swan of Avon	A	Homer
2	The Swan of the Meander	B	John Taylor
3	The Mantuan Swan	C	Francesco Algarotti
4	The Swan of the Thames	D	Shakespeare
5	The Swan of Padua	E	Virgil
6	The Swan of Usk	F	Anna Seward
7	The Swan of Lichfield	G	Henry Vaughan

Answers: 1.D 2.A 3.E 4.B 5.C 6.G 7.F

May

Bluebell magic

ABOUT the month of May, the poet Milton wrote:

> *Hail bounteous May! that dost inspire*
> *Mirth, and youth, and warm desire.*

Well, yes, and we all share with Milton a desire to welcome May - a month associated with sunshine and flowers. It is traditionally the Merry Month, and May Day marks the beginning of summer. The month of May is full of pagan rituals symbolising earth, fire, water, life and death and to this extent is perhaps Nature's miniature picture of the entire yearly cycle.

Not only Milton, but Longfellow too praised the month of May. It was Longfellow who, in his *Journal*, said:

> *The word May is a perfumed word. It is an illuminated initial. It means youth, love, song, and all that is beautiful in life.*

Talking of things beautiful, long ago country girls on May Day used to wash their faces with the dew of the morning to improve complexions. It is, in some places, one of the very few old May Day customs still observed but, early as I am out on May mornings, I have never seen a damsel scooping up the dew in the meadow beside the cottage!

This is the month to appreciate one of the loveliest of all sights in the English countryside – carpets of Bluebells under woodland trees.

Although Bluebells flower from April to early June, my family usually leaves it until about the middle of May before we visit some Leicestershire woodland which we know will by then be covered with blue. For me the passing of the years has in no way lessened my pleasure in 'going Bluebelling' and even if the weather on the chosen day is not too tempting then I remember that bit of country wisdom which tells us that there is no such thing as *bad* weather; only *different* sorts of weather.

On me, a Bluebell wood had a deep emotional effect as if, by some strange magic, adult years are for a few fleeting moments blotted out and I see again as a child sees. In this reverie I share the Lincolnshire poet Tennyson's thoughts that Bluebells are *'like a blue sky breaking up through the earth'*, and it was for such reason that I chose for the colour cover of this book a picture of bluebells in a woodland glade and where, in a breeze, the leaves and smaller branches of trees seem to be doing a ballet. Such a scene makes me doubly sure that there is nothing wrong with Nature and the world except that people cause. (The cover photograph was taken in woods near the Lickey Hills, not far from the City of Birmingham.)

I hope that what I am saying about Bluebells will produce in your mind's eye a picture of their innocent and perfumed beauty since creating pictures like these is – as the BBC's Mr Lawrie Bloomfield so kindly says of me in his introduction – my main objective in broadcasting (and I particularly keep in mind the fact that 83 per cent of our entire population live in urban and suburban built-up surroundings).

The Tennyson phrase quoted is powerfully descriptive; so is the following written by the priest and poet Gerard Manley Hopkins in his *Journal* for 1871: Bluebells, he said, 'come in falls of sky-colour washing the brows and slacks of the ground with vein-blue (a reminiscence of Shakespeare in *Cymbeline*.) The stalks rub and click... making a brittle rub and jostle like the noise of a hurdle strained by leaning against... I caught, as well as I could while my companions talked, the Greek rightness of their beauty, the lovely gracious bidding one to another or all one way, the level or stage or shire of colour they make hanging in the air a foot above the grass...'

If what most of us call Bluebells are more correctly termed Wild Hyacinths (or in Latin, *Endymion nonscriptus*) and Harebells are the true Bluebells of Scotland renowned in music, there are nevertheless a number of attractive local names for Bluebells: in Derbyshire and Nottinghamshire children used to call the flowers Cuckoo's Stockings and – as the Mayor of Casterbridge would have said in Thomas Hardy's country – they are Skeggles or Goosey-Ganders.

As for the actual picking of Bluebells (and in very small amounts I may say), I was taught as a child not to pull the stems upwards with that long white piece at the end but rather to snap the flowers off at ground level, otherwise the bulb would be spoiled for the following year. But apparently not so. Botanists now say that the real damage is done by too much heavy treading of the Bluebell's leaves. If this is so then it is another example of too many people destroying the very things they go to see, as indeed is happening to hills and dales in the National Parks where footpaths are being worn away by thousands of walkers.

Hawthorn recipes

BY THE MIDDLE of May, hedgerows and coppice have quite a number of flowers and most trees have opened their leaf and flower buds.

I find it surprising that many people seem to think that flowering trees are confined to such very obvious species whose flowers one cannot miss seeing – Wild Cherry, Crab Apple, Mountain Ash and the familiar cultivated flowering trees in town parks. So often it is not realised that, for instance, the Holly deserves a close inspection at this time of year. It does have flowers even though they are made very inconspicuous by the glossy, dark green foliage surrounding them. Look carefully at an established Holly and you will see flower buds clustering round the stems and a bit later bursting into delicate, wax-like cream coloured flowers.

What a lovely sight country hedgerows are just now, full of pink and white May Blossom – the name commonly given to the scented flowers of Hawthorn, and never have I seen Hawthorn (and Holly, come to that) more blossom-laden than in this year of 1983. There is more blossom than leaves on some big Hawthorns making it look as though the trees are covered with snow, and from this bumper crop of flowers our Bees have made some of the best flavoured honey (not even excluding Heather honey) that we have ever taken from the hives.

Hedges of Hawthorn are of course a man-made feature of our landscape, planted mainly in the eighteenth century during the great land enclosure movement to prevent farm livestock from straying. But apart from its use as hedging, the Hawthorn shelters plants from bad weather and acts as a nursery for seedlings of trees like the Oak and Ash.

Hawthorn (a word which comes from the Anglo-Saxon 'haegthron', meaning hedge-thorn) is long-lived, sometimes up to 200 years.

Hawthorn folklore abounds – so do various ways of eating either the leaves or the berries. For instance, how about a Hawthorn suet roll? I can give you my grandmother's old Midlands' recipe: first make a light suet crust, season well with pepper and salt, then roll it out long and thin. Next, cover the surface smoothly with the green Hawthorn leaf buds, patting them down lightly. Follow this by cutting a rasher of bacon into fine strips and lay these on the Hawthorn before moistening the edges of the crust, rolling it up tightly and sealing the edges as you go. Now you are ready to tie the roll into a cloth and boil or steam for at least an hour before cutting and serving in thick slices, with gravy. So tasty is this suet roll that one Derbyshire village I know used to hold a Spring 'Hawthorn Dinner' each year. One only hopes the gatherers of the sprouting Hawthorn buds did not disturb any nests of Long-Tailed Tits since Hawthorn bushes are one of their favourite places for nesting.

Or how about trying Hawthorn brandy liqueur made from the May Blossom? This is how to make the liqueur: cut the almond-scented Hawthorn flowers when in their full aroma, using scissors and take only the flower heads – not the small stems. Pack the flowers into a bottle with a wide mouth, shaking the blossom down rather loosely – do not press or bruise the Hawthorn flowers. Next shake a little fine sugar (two tablespoonful to a pint bottle) over the flowers, fill up with brandy and cork tightly. Put the bottle into full sunshine until warmed through; then store in a warm, dark cupboard.

During the first few weeks shake the bottle gently so that the sugar is dissolved and evenly distributed. After that, let the liqueur stand unmoved for three months before decanting gently into smaller bottles and cork securely. And there you have a fine, home-made liqueur.

The lobed leaves of the Hawthorn, very variable in size and shape, are a favourite food of horses and cattle who would demolish the hedges that confine them to the fields but for the Hawthorn's sharp spines. Country children call the fresh, bright green leaf-buds 'bread and cheese' and are often the first wild vegetable they eat. These leaf-buds have a nutty taste and make an excellent addition to potato and beetroot salads (one teacupful of Hawthorn buds to four times this quantity of potato salad).

In May, the blossom comes in clusters on unclipped Hawthorn bushes, never on close-trimmed hedges however tidy and neat they look on the farms. The red haws, which come in the autumn, are useful for making Haw Jelly – quite splendid to eat with cream cheese, if you can collect them before birds such as the Thrush, members of the Tit family and our winter visitors the Fieldfare and Redwing get at them. Wood mice and other little animals are also quite partial to Hawthorn berries.

The May Queen

AS TO THE folklore of this tree you may know that the custom of crowning a May Queen and dancing round the Maypole are linked with May Day as a festival of fertility. In France it used to be a May Day fertility custom to place branches of Hawthorn outside the windows of young ladies since the musky scent of the blossom was thought to be sexually suggestive.

The 'wicked' connotations of May Day were disliked by the more fervent Puritans of the sixteenth and seventeenth centuries and before that, in the early fourteenth century, the Church attempted to sanctify Hawthorn rather than oppose its fertility beliefs. Hawthorn, as carved foliage, entered the churches – a good example is the chapter house at Southwell Minster in Nottinghamshire, where heads wreathed in Hawthorn are portrayed along with other May Day magical plants including Oak, Ivy, Cinquefoil, Buttercup and Maple.

Hawthorn was thought to be supernaturally powerful against many evils, including witches. In Ireland, lone Hawthorn trees belong to the fairies – thus the Victorian poet William Allingham in his poem *The Fairies* ('up the airy mountain, down the rushy glen' etc) declares:

> *By the craggy hillside*
> *Through the mosses bare*
> *They have planted thorntrees*
> *For pleasure here and there.*
>
> *Is any man so daring*
> *As dig them up in spite,*
> *He shall find their sharpest thorns*
> *In his bed at night.*

Indeed, Irish fairies are said to meet at the Hawthorn trees, or live under them. Cut the lone thorn and it may bleed or scream! By an English rhyme

> *Under a thorn*
> *Our Saviour was born*

the power of Hawthorn is made Christian, and the fame of the Thorn in Somerset is associated with Hawthorn as the material of Christ's Crown of Thorns.

I like the numerous and picturesque local names for Hawthorn. Here are just a few: in Buckinghamshire they call it the azzy-tree; in Yorkshire, hag-bush; heg-peg in Gloucestershire; and hipperty-haw in Shropshire. The fruits of Hawthorn have some odd names too: agarve in Sussex; bird's eagle in Cheshire, and pixie-bear in Dorset.

The Cuckoos and Swallows are with us by early May, back once again from wintering in warm Africa. From early April onwards some people seem compelled to write to the newspapers asking whether the date on which they first heard a Cuckoo is a record. And this year these letters have come from such odd-sounding places as Piddletrenthide near Dorchester, Pratt's Bottom in Kent, and Peas Pottage in Sussex. It gets tedious, but I admit that there *is* something pleasant about hearing that first Cuckoo call; it means Spring is really here, not just a calendar date.

There is a lot of nonsense talked about dates on which people say they first heard a Cuckoo. Officially the arrival of the Cuckoo, even in the South of England, has rarely been observed before the 6th April. By the middle of that month, but again only in the South, there are a fair number of these birds about. In Sussex they talk of April 14th being 'Cuckoo Day'.

When you hear your first Cuckoo partly depends on weather conditions, cold or otherwise, but errors of identification often explain very early so-called sightings. The bird some hear and think is a Cuckoo is nothing of the kind: more likely a Collared Dove, a bird which breeds right through from early February till November and whose *coo-cooo-cuk* call is easily mistaken for that of the Cuckoo. A farmer neighbour of mine has kept a Nature and farm diary meticulously for the past 25 years and the earliest he has ever recorded a Cuckoo was the last week in April, in 1972.

Perhaps because the Cuckoo is the accepted announcer of the arrival of Spring, it is considered a lucky bird. If your first Cuckoo call is heard from the right-hand side, or from in front of where you are, this was long considered to be a sign of good luck – but if you hear the first Cuckoo from the left, or from behind, then you could be in for some trouble! What a lot of nonsense to be sure, but never mind... in Scotland you are supposed to turn over the money in your pocket as soon as you hear the Cuckoo, and make a wish; while in German country districts a Cuckoo call from the south foretells, in some strange way, a good butter year!

Although Cuckoos' eggs have been found in the nests of over fifty different species of bird, they seem to prefer Hedge Sparrows, Wagtails, Warblers and Meadow Pipits (incidentally, the Welsh word for Meadow Pipit is *gwas-y-gog,* meaning the Cuckoo's servant). A remarkable thing, but Cuckoos' eggs often vary in colour and markings to match the eggs of the chosen foster-parents. I once found a Cuckoo's egg of pale blue among the smaller but equally blue eggs of a Hedge Sparrow, whereas the normal colour of a Cuckoo's egg is greenish or reddish grey.

The young Cuckoo hatches out after twelve days and by the time it is only thirty hours old the intruding baby begins to throw overboard the rightful occupants of the nest by means of a hollow in its back which acts like a scoop. And what always strikes me as being so odd is that although the small foster-parent birds mob the Cuckoo when she is prospecting for a nest, as soon as the Cuckoo egg is in a nest no attempt is made to reject it – or even shove the intruding Cuckoo out of the nest when it is hatched. Once a young Cuckoo has got the nest entirely to itself it clamours for more and ever more food until, quite soon, it is bigger than the foster-parents. I once watched Hedge Sparrows standing on a young Cuckoo's back to feed it. When it is born a Cuckoo weighs just half an ounce, but in only three weeks it weighs 50 times that amount.

May is also the time to watch out for the many colourful insects joining the butterflies and bees. By mid-May I usually see the first of the bold red and brown Cinnabar Moths searching for Ragwort plants on which to lay their yellow eggs. And there are plenty of vivid coloured Ladybirds around. I suppose one reason why I have seen so many Ladybirds this particular year, is that, like farmers and others, I have been keeping a wary eye open for the dreaded Colorado Beetle which sometimes come into this country with imported vegetables. This black and yellow striped insect, often called the Potato Beetle, can devastate a crop in a short time. Mistaking a Laydbird for a Colorado Beetle should not happen – but does; you can be sure it is a Colorado if the coloured stripes run from front to back rather than *across* the insect. And here is another warning: if bright pink or red coloured *grubs* are found eating potato leaves they are definitely of the Colorado Beetle since there is no similar grub in Britain that feeds on potato leaves.

In the Cowslips

COWSLIPS: there, surely, is one of the greatest joys of May. I love all wild flowers but perhaps best of all the dainty yellow Cowslip. But alas, this plant is becoming scarce, largely through the ploughing and re-seeding of farm grazing land and the spraying of weed killers on roadside verges.

Along some stretches of road and in certain counties one can still see clumps of Cowslips here and there, but there are nowadays very, very few farm fields polka-dotted with these flowers as was once common enough. In this respect how fortunate I am to know just one such Cowslip field in Leicestershire, rightly officially protected and classified as being of Special Scientific Interest (and here let me say how grateful we are to the farmer concerned for leaving this permanent pasture unploughed). Although I often talk in my broadcasts about the Cowslips and other flowers in this particular field I do not, for conservation reasons, reveal its whereabouts – the more so since one of my daughters found several species of Orchid growing in the field and they, too, are worth safeguarding!

The Cowslip is now a protected plant and well deserves to be for its beauty of form and colour but the time was when thousands of flower heads were gathered in May and June to make wine; and some country folk even used to make Cowslip ointment, claimed to remove facial spots and wrinkles. So, even if you find some Cowslips, no greedy picking, please.

One of the most evocative references to Cowslips that I know in poetry comes from D.H. Lawrence:

> *You amid the bog-end's yellow incantation,*
> *You sitting in the cowslips of the meadow above,*
> *Me, your shadow on the bog-flame flowery may-blobs,*
> *Me full length in the cowslips, muttering you love;*
> *You, your soul like a lady-smock, lost, evanescent,*
> *You with your face all rich, like the sheen on a dove!*

The nodding flowers of the Cowslip, resembling perhaps a bunch of keys, gave rise to a legend heard in Northern Europe that St Peter let a bunch of keys drop when he was told that a duplicated key to Heaven had been made. Where the keys fell, so this old Prussian tale goes, the Cowslip grew. 'Bunch of Keys' is one of many local names for Cowslips in our countryside, including Cooslop in Lincolnshire, Paigle in most Midland counties, Tisty-Tosty in the West Country and *dagrau Mair* (Mary's Tears) in Wales.

In the Middle Ages it was customary to plant Yew trees in churchyards to ensure a supply of the best timber for making bows (arrows, for the use of) since - at least in those days - the trees would be safe from spivs flogging under-weight loads of wood for aged cottagers' fires. From Suffolk there now comes the admirable suggestion that we should use churchyards and cemeteries to preserve endangered wild flowers at the same time as beautifying these necessary places - why not indeed? Proof of how good the idea is comes from a Bury St Edmunds' cemetery, this year carpeted with Cowslips.

On this subject of wildlife conservation in churchyards, this year a Women's Institute survey in Lincolnshire led to the discovery of a nest containing twelve eggs and built of dried grasses beneath a tombstone in the old burial ground on the hill at Woolsthorpe-by-Belvoir. Two of the WI ladies asked me to go and see the nest hidden in the Nettles and Cow Parsley and it was, as I thought from their earlier description, that of a Partridge. But alas, a Rat or perhaps a Magpie, had been there and only eight eggs remained - all cold. But I thought how pleasant for Thomas Isherwood who was buried there in February 1837 that a Partridge should choose to nest beneath his tombstone on which is carved - 'Ever faithfull in his duties and unwearied in his attentions, he faithfully discharged his trust as groom of the chambers to his noble master His Grace the Duke of Rutland by whom for his good conduct he was highly esteemed.'

With jar and net

FEW THINGS I have talked about in nearly three years of my BBC Radio Lincolnshire country broadcasts have brought me more letters and telephone calls from listeners than the scarcity in recent years of Stickleback fish and Frogs.

When I was a boy catching Sticklebacks (or bandies as we called them) and gathering Frog-spawn to watch the Tadpoles hatch out in the home glass tank was a regular school holiday pastime, using mother's old stockings as nets! Now it is not at all easy to find these pretty little fish or the Frogs, something which is usually put down to pollution of water courses by farm chemicals. Maybe, but some of my radio listeners believe the blame must also be shared by water authorities and their 'obsession' (to quote one correspondent from Market Rasen) with constant dredging to remove Reed Mace and other aquatic plant life from our rivers.

My country 'bush telegraph' informs me of a few ponds where Sticklebacks can still be seen; indeed one listener complained to me of fishing all day but catching nothing more than a solitary Perch because shoals of 'little nuisances' (he meant Sticklebacks) would keep taking his bait of worms and maggots.

It is during the Sticklebacks' breeding season from March to July that these fish change colour quite remarkably. They are normally blue-black or dark green, with paler colours beneath, but in their Spring dress the female fish goes a pale yellowish tinge, while the male shows off with a brilliant orange throat and belly, a green back and sparkling blue eyes. I do not think there is any more striking breeding colouration than a Stickleback in the entire fish world.

With these attractive colours, and an elaborate courtship ritual, the male Stickleback lures a female into a nest he himself has built among the reeds at the water's edge. His nest is not easy to find: the best way is to sit quietly for a while just watching male Sticklebacks swimming around. Their habit is to keep visiting the nest to check that everything is normal and to the careful observer this will soon reveal the whereabouts of a nest. Another give-away sign is the angry raising of the spines on a male's back preparatory to attack when a rival fish comes near the nest.

The design of the nest is the most intriguing thing about this species. First, the male Stickleback scoops out a hollow in the shallow water bed of the pond; next he arranges bits and pieces of wood around the hollow, binding the materials together with sticky threads ejected from his kidneys. The finished job looks like a tube, closed at one end. The Stickleback forces a female into the tube and there keeps her prisoner until she lays about ten eggs. Then a most remarkable thing happens: this first love affair ends with the female opening up the sealed end of the tube, thus converting the nest into a tunnel into which the male Stickleback promptly continues to lure other females to add to the few eggs already there until, finally, there are about 80,000 eggs in this 'tunnel of love'. In due course this staggering total means a lot of fish dinners for those creatures and birds who feed on small fry, like Pike and Perch, waterside animals and Kingfishers.

As a lad I found Sticklebacks did well, even raising their young, in a home aquarium. If you do find and catch any of these fish give them plenty of oxygenating weed and, of course, use only pond or rain water.

Frog-spawn – now here is another country lad's joy to find at this time of the year; boys have been collecting Frog-spawn for generations – or (like Sticklebacks) *did* until recent years. To be quite accurate, the Frog breeding business started last month, when Frogs could be heard croaking away quite loudly. One female Frog will lay as many as 3,000 eggs – and this is just as well considering that from all these eggs only a few Tadpoles will survive to Frog stage; all the rest will be eaten by fish, Newts and water birds to all of which Tadpoles are a delicacy on the menu.

At first, when the female Frog has laid her eggs, these sink to the bottom of the pond and float to the surface only when the protective coat of jelly swells to form Frog-spawn. If you should find any of this floating near the edge of some clean pond this month it should by now be showing the little rolled up Tadpoles inside getting ready to emerge by the end of the month.

I happened, late one May, to be passing one of those fascinating fishing tackle shops and, as I always do, I just had to take a quick look at all those spanking new fishing rods and the rest of the colourful paraphernalia in the window. I saw plenty of customers going in and out of the shop and thought to myself how very nicely the business must be doing! Then it dawned on me just why trade was so brisk – the anglers were getting ready for the start of the coarse fishing season early next month.

Each year two or three keen fishermen will already be installed around our lakesides and on the canal by midnight on the day the close season ends, all kitted-up for the very first few minutes of new fishing. I always hope the anglers will remember that fishing, like any other sport, has its rules: apart from the technique of how to catch fish there is the question of showing good manners to landowners or authorities who allow them to fish their waters or roam the field pathways. Never leave litter around in the countryside; do not, please, walk through growing crops; and do not leave fishing hooks and nylon lying around – such stuff can kill birds and injure farm animals.

Dawn chorus

ONCE upon a time in my professional life I was on duty between 8 p.m. and 5 o'clock in the morning – and one of its very few advantages, as far as I was concerned, was that it enabled me at about this time of the year to enjoy the dawn chorus of wild birds when the early morning train returned me home.

The third week in May is the ideal time for this exhilarating experience because by then all, or almost all, of the summer migrants are back with us; what is more, it seems that all the different birds wake up at the same time for a few days and the chorus includes such species as the Blackcap, Whitethroat, Redstart and, of course, the superb Nightingale – all adding their music to that of our resident songsters like the Thrush, Blackbird, Robin and Finches.

In those days I was living further south. The Nightingale was sure to be heard, and what a delight it was. The popularity of its song is to some extent due to the fact that the countryman, lying in bed at night or just before it gets light in the morning, can hear a Nightingale singing very clearly because the other birds are silent. The Nightingale, however, does not sing *only* at night as many think but its daytime song is drowned by the singing of other birds.

If you want to hear a Nightingale 'first hand' you will have to make your pilgrimage, even supposing you know where to go, before the end of May. Their song period ends when the young are hatched early in June. What is not often realised is that there is no particular need to be ultra quiet – in fact, if there *is* a Nightingale about any disturbing noise will often startle it into song. A Nightingale we hear locally sings away on a rubbish tip not a quarter of a mile off the village pub with a noisy car park.

Come August the young Nightingales are off to warmer lands, but the parents stay on a bit longer to complete their moult. Some ornithologists say that the Nightingale migrates alone rather than in flocks like other birds, but against this theory I rather like an old newspaper report of rows of Nightingales resting, during their flight south, along the whole length of coastline at Brighton *under the bathing machines* (times change, do they not!)

It is not only at Brighton that times have changed. Since I was a boy, the commemorative occasion of Oak Apple Day on the 29th May seems to have disappeared from the calendar. Nowadays, one never sees any children, let alone adults, wearing – as they used to do – an Oak apple or a sprig of Oak leaves in their buttonholes, and perhaps you have never even heard of the custom.

The wearing of Oak apples (or, more correctly, Oak galls) on the 29th, was to commemorate that eventful day in history when King Charles the Second escaped from his enemies after the Battle of Worcester in 1651 by hiding in an Oak tree at Boscobel, in Shropshire. The story was thought by some to be untrue since the foliage of an Oak tree at this time of early summer is not advanced enough for the leaves to conceal a child, let alone a man. Agreed, but even so the story *is* true and I can tell you just why the disbelievers are in error. Charles the Second was *born* on May 29th in 1630 and it is on that account that his adventure in the Oak tree is, or rather was, celebrated on the 29th. The escape from his pursuers after the Battle of Worcester took place on September 3rd, 1651, at a time of the year when an Oak tree is in full leaf and could certainly hide a man; in fact the Boscobel Oak hid not one man but two – the King himself and one of his army colonels.

Years ago there was often a school holiday on Oak Apple Day and I can recall as a child chanting for the benefit of the village schoolmaster...

> *Twentyninth of May, Oak Apple Day,*
> *If you don't give us a holiday*
> *We'll all run away.*

In those days if we could not find an Oak apple a sprig of leaves would do, but to be without *either* of the loyal emblems meant one was liable to be beaten with nettles (provided it was before twelve noon) and I suppose that is why May 29th was sometimes called Oak-and-Nettle Day.

Longfellow was asked when he was an old man how he could write so many happy childlike things, full of joy and wonder. He replied that a 200 years old pear tree 'still bears fruit not to be distinguished from a young tree in flavour'.

June

Bees in our bonnets

IT IS SAID, 'Spring is the season of hope and promise, but summer is the time of fulfilment'. That fulfilment begins this month and Nature's gifts are here in plenty. Early summer skies are one of the sights of June, even if the weather does not always warrant the description 'flaming June'.

Remember that old saying 'Ne're cast a clout till May is out' but, truth to tell, its origin has nothing to do with the name of that month. May was the name of a young lady of ill-repute who lived in the Shoreditch area of East London in the mid-1840s. May was what Victorians called 'a fourpenny drab' (pre-inflation days, of course) and she frequently slept out in a Shoreditch park. She was a cunning old soak and reckoned it was more comfortable to spend each winter in jail, coming out well fed (and rested) in early June when the weather was warmer... and that is how we got the saying 'Ne're cast a clout till May is out (the words 'of jail' having been dropped at some time).

But now – Bees, and a very demanding and important part of our way of cottage life they are. My wife does all the work and it is only when I am called in to give some minor help that these wonderful insects cause me any trouble – not surprisingly since, unlike my wife in protective clothing, I have to face any attack more or less defenceless. Anyway, what do a few bee-stings matter – good for rheumatism, so they say.

There are only five hives in the orchard beside the River Devon but even so that means we have something up to a quarter of a million Bees flying around and working for us. (Incidentally should you ever be our way and notice an odd sign on a cottage gate reading not just the usual 'Beware of Dog' but 'Beware of Dog and Bees' you can be sure it is our place.) We find undesirable callers are more often put off by the fear of Bees than they are of a dog!

Wonderful things, Bees. Did you know, for instance, that there are something like 250 different types in our countryside, although fewer than 30 of them live and work together in colonies like domestic honey Bees. Most are solitary insects nesting in various sorts of holes and providing a source of food for their eggs – but leaving these to hatch out alone. By contrast, the honey Bees kept in hives are very social little creatures with a most sophisticated system of communal life: incidentally, there is no finer way to see this in action then to visit the City of Nottingham's Natural History Museum at Wollaton Hall – galleries on the first floor are devoted to insects, including an observation beehive and a live colony of Wood Ants. The silviculturist and diarist

John Evelyn (1620-1706) had the same idea – he kept Bees in glass 'so you may see the Bees making their honey and combs mighty pleasantly.'

Domestic Bees are, it seems, heading for a great technological future as surveyors, revealing areas for possible mines and locating sites of industrial pollution. It was recently proved that small quantities of zinc, copper, lead, gold and silver can show up in pollen; with beehives spread around a pattern of mineral deposits can be built up. Detection of polluted soil comes from the examination of pollen from plants which have grown there.

Occasionally we are lucky enough to obtain what every beekeeper prays for – capturing a swarm of Bees early in the season. Bees are very expensive to buy and this is why countrymen say that:

> A swarm of Bees in May is worth a load of hay;
> A swarm of Bees in June is worth a silver spoon;
> But a swarm in July isn't worth a fly!

The reasons behind this old country jingle are, of course, that if you can secure a free swarm early on and get it into a hive complete, then those thousands of Bees will be happy gathering honey all the rest of the summer. By mid-summer there is obviously less working time left before the autumn shut-down. I said Bees are nowadays expensive to buy – proof of this came abruptly upon my wife this summer when she telephoned a would-be seller to ask 'how much?' Expressing some amazement at the asking price, the reply was 'Now look here madam, gone are the days when silly old men sold bees for a few pounds to little old ladies who then graciously gave the honey away for all manner of good causes.' Quite so, but the deal was off.

The last time we were lucky enough to get a free swarm happened when our village motor engineer friend telephoned asking if, as an urgent favour, my wife could remove a swarm from his garden raspberry canes. I was not surprised to be told that he and his wife were worried about their baby in her pram in the garden sunshine – angry Bees were buzzing all over the place, quite apart from the tightly-packed lot clinging to about three-feet of wooden post surrounding the raspberry canes.

With us on this rescue operation was that renowned East Midlands beekeeper Mrs Annie Stubley (often in our village referred to as 'the Queen Bee'!) and both she and my wife were, of course, properly protected from stings with helmets and all the rest of the beekeeper's outfit; even so, such was the difficulty of this particular removal job, a few Bees managed to penetrate my wife's overalls and sting her quite severely. The reason the job was difficult was because the Bees were not all hanging together in a neat ball on a tree trunk as they usually do in a swarm; this lot was spread out all up the wooden post.

After two hours' struggle our friend's garden was even fuller of Bees, very angry indeed at being disturbed from the rest of the swarm – and there were mighty few in the box! We knew then that until the queen was inside the box we should do no good. So, after Mrs Stubley had brushed as many bees as possible into the box, the campaign was called off until the following day – a Sunday, hoping that the queen had been secured and the rest of the Bees would follow. The better the day, the better the deed, as the saying goes and, sure enough, on the Sunday our luck was in. By the time we returned to the scene on the Sunday evening all was peaceful... no more angry insects zooming overhead; all were safely gathered in and were soon in a new hive bringing in the honey.

People who have seen a swarm of Bees often ask me 'what makes them do it?' The answer is that it happens when the old queen in a colony (and there can be anything up to 60,000 bees in a hive) has to give way to a new and younger queen. The old queen flies off, with half the hive's worker Bees following her, to set up a new home. In this way the survival of the species is ensured.

Bees depend for their living on flowers. They can cover over a square mile a day and a colony can visit more than a thousand flowers in that time. In their turn, flowers to a very large extent depend for their survival on pollination, through the help of Bees, butterflies and other insects. And this is where the colours of flowers come in. Different colours attract different insects – the Tortoiseshell butterfly goes for yellow or blue flowers whereas the Large White butterfly ignores anything except purple or violet. Bees cannot see red, but they can distinguish between yellow and blue – and they are also sensitive to ultraviolet rays which we cannot see, with the result that some flowers must look quite a different colour to the Bees from what *we* think they are!

June is the month in which many wild flowers reach their peak: the Ox-Eye Daisy, Honeysuckle, Charlock and scores of others. It is a bonanza month for Bees – particularly since farmers have increased the acreage of Oilseed Rape.

All insects are there for the purpose of pollen exchange and so fertilising plants to produce seed. But there are a few flowers of little use to Bees – flowers like the Field Poppy, Wild Roses and the gorgeous red Peonies in the garden offer no nectar but lots of pollen instead and for this reason are dependent on pollen-eating beetles. Conversely, some trees – in particular the Lime – are great nectar producers. The foliage of the Lime is often shiny with honeydew from the masses of aphids which infest the tree and it is their secretions, plus nectar, which rain down and so deposit a sooty mould on anything below (never park your car under a Lime tree.)

Month of Roses

ABOVE all else, June is the month of Roses – in gardens and in country lanes. The Wild Rose has been England's national emblem since the Wars of the Roses in the fifteenth century, the red rose for Lancaster and the white of York. Almost everyone knows that the briar, or Dog Rose, is the parent of many of our garden roses, but not so well known is the fact that there are more than a hundred types of *wild* roses. I find it a pleasing thought that when the Romans first came to England so many centuries ago they are said to have sent a message back to Italy saying that their newly-discovered country of England was 'a land of roses'.

The Wild Roses you are most likely to see are the Dog Rose with its mainly pink flowers in the hedgerows just now and, a little later, the much rarer white flowered Wild Rose in woods and shady places, the proper name of which is the Field Rose, despite being found mostly in woods.

The Dog Rose was so named because medieval apothecaries (and, with good reason, you will find them often quoted in my book!) maintained that an extract from the root of this species (*Rosa canina*, of course) cured the bad effects of being bitten by mad dogs. The colour of the Dog Rose can vary from the usual pink to white, the same colour as the Field Rose; the only sure way to tell one from the other is that not only is the Field Rose unscented but the styles bearing the long stigma on which pollen is deposited, are joined together in the centre of the flowers, whereas in the Dog Rose the styles are not so joined and the stigma is short.

Looking at these June roses reminds me of the joys to come in the Autumn when the bushes are loaded with scarlet hips (or cat-jugs as I have heard them called in Yorkshire). For instance, making Rose Hip syrup, which contains more Vitamin C than other fruit or vegetable – in fact, four times as much a much as that expensive bottled Black Currant juice and twenty times as much as oranges.

It is simple enough to make the syrup. Just gather a good quantity of

Rose Hips and mince them into three pints of boiling water. When the hips are reduced to a soft pulp let the stuff drain through a linen bag before returning the residue to the saucepan and boiling down until you have about a pint of juice. To this, add a pound of sugar and boil for five minutes. Bottle-up when cool and that is all there is to it.

Rose Hip wine is another good thing, and for this powerful concoction pick a gallon measure of hips and to these add two ounces of root ginger, two sliced oranges, two sliced lemons and a half a gallon of water. Boil the lot until the hips are tender and then allow to stand for three days, stirring daily. Next, strain and add about a pound of sugar, the juice of a lemon and a little yeast. Pour into a cask or open bottles but do not cork up for at least three days. It is tempting to drink this lovely pink coloured wine right away, but take my advice and leave it alone for three months.

Before even waiting for the hips to be ready in the autumn, rose petal jam is something you can enjoy making whilst the roses are in summer bloom. As you gather wild rose petals (or old-fashioned Damask garden roses will also do) put them in a deep earthenware bowl, squeezing a little lemon juice over the petals before covering the crock. To each pound of petals add half a pound of sugar and half a pound of honey. All you have to do then is to add a little water and boil gently until the jam sets. Delicious. Just try some rose petal jam with yoghurt and see what you think.

Country scents

I SUPPOSE that of all the scents that mark the different seasons of the countryman's year none is more familiar or more impressionable than that of new-mown hay. For most of us it has more nostalgic power than any of the smells, sights and sounds which impressed us as children.

A whiff of clean, cut hay is the season's most potent scent – but nowadays, because of mechanised silage making, it is not so often that one gets the pleasure of smelling newly-mown hay, swathe upon swathe of it lying for a day in sun and wind; then, in turning them over with a fork or a scaler, getting that delicious and even stronger smell than at actual cutting time.

Along with haytime come the flowers on the Elder bushes which Nature has so kindly linked with the hayfield in both time and place. Of the Elder it is said that 'Summer is never established until they are in flower and it ends only when the Elderberries are purple ripe'. Certainly the Elder blossoms when the meadows are ready for mowing and so it is that the scent is mingled with the hay – altogether, for me and most other country lads, a haunting fragrance we can never forget. (Incidentally, a bunch of dried Elder flowers makes an excellent insect repellant in the larder.)

Meadowsweet is another unforgettable country scent, and it is not unlike newly mown hay. This plant, often called Queen of the Meadows, is probably seen at its best on the edges of fields, ponds and streams. Meadowsweet has a 'heady' scent and years ago I can remember my sister being told not to have the cream-coloured flowers in her bedroom or she would wake up with a nasty headache! The crushed flowers of Meadowsweet have the freshness of carbolic, an antiseptic smell I enjoy although I know not everyone does. I suppose it was because of this clean smell that in the Middle Ages pieces of Meadowsweet were strewn among the rushes used to cover floors.

The coastline

I HAVE BEEN eulogising about the *scents* of June, but the *sounds* of this month impress me too, and to hear these at their best you should go down to the sea. Try visiting not the level sands, nice as they may be for the family, but find a spit of land on which the breakers roll and deposit shingle since that is the best place to get good sound effects.

I know just such a spot on the East Coast where I can walk gently among the nests of Ringed Plovers and Black-Headed Gulls, even if they do shriek at me being there. After a while these birds stop being so aggressive and one can hear the lighter notes of the Little Tern, the happy sound of Oyster Catchers and even the soft sound of a Sandwich Tern, the bird with the unmistakeable trade mark of a yellow-tipped black bill.

The seashore is a harsh world for birds since it is more subject to extremes than any other environment. The U.K. coastline itself ranges from sheer cliffs to gently sloping sands and mudflats and in Lincolnshire the coast is swept by icy east winds in winter. Despite the cold, the constantly changing world of the seashore has an abundant supply of plant, bird and animal species. When the tide is high shoals of fish visit the shore and, as the tide ebbs, their place is taken by wading birds and it is they, and the sea itself, which make the sounds of a lonely coastline so attractive.

Watching the different kinds of birds feeding alongside each other it is easy enough to see how body structure has been adapted to ensure that they are not endlessly competing one with another for the same food. Birds like the Curlew and Black-Tailed Godwit can wade out into the water on stilt-like legs – they can also probe deep into mud with their long bills. The medium-sized birds, with shorter legs and bills, are restricted to shallow water while birds like the tiny Dunlin tirelessly glean a living from the edge – one of my delights is to watch these pretty little birds run away up the beach, rather like a group of children when an incoming wave threatens to swamp them.

Another June sound I always delight in comes, if I am lucky, when I walk along the canal towpath. It is the chirping of a Grasshopper Warbler, a sound similar to that made by the Grasshopper and Cricket insects – or even similar to the clicking noise when a fishing rod is being wound in. I have heard this Warbler quite often but very, very rarely have I seen it – I suppose because the Grasshopper Warbler, very much a waterside frequenter, remains hidden most of the time and does not fly out from the reeds and surrounding bushes as one walks by. As a boy, I used to spend countless hours searching for a Grasshopper Warbler's nest but was largely defeated by the fact that these birds hide their nests at the end of a tunnel-like approach, so making them very difficult to find.

On warm evenings at the end of this month and into July – the breeding season – there appear little yellowish-green 'beacons' in the laneside verges and on heath land. These lights are signals emitted by Glow-worms and, despite the name, they are beetles not worms. Only the females can 'switch on the lights' and the magic glow comes not from their eyes but from the last three segments of their bodies. I have watched them carefully and the odd thing is that only the male Glow-worm can fly – perhaps that privilege is to make up for not being able to light up to attract a partner!

Very recently the Glow-worm has started shedding light in a dramatic and unexpected way. First, scientists at Sussex University discovered the make-up of the chemicals in Glow-worms and how to make synthetic versions of them. Next, at the Welsh National School of Medicine, these compounds were linked with other substances to produce light-emitting antibodies which, when mixed with human blood, can identify people carrying diseases such as spina bifida – as well as detecting cannabis and other drugs in the blood.

Another remarkable thing about Glow-worms occurred in 1891 when a tiny but recognisable photograph was taken with the eye of a male Glow-worm being used as a camera lens. The picture was taken during a series of experiments to discover how animals can see – and of course, the male Glow-worm's eyes were particularly suitable since they are very large to enable them to detect those tiny lights put out by ladies during the July breeding season.

Owl on the 'phone

FROM Glow-worms to Owls – very much a species of wild life having, for me, an irresistible appeal. On some June evenings we have had a splendid view of a Little Owl who has obligingly taken to using the cottage telephone wires as an observation post. No need even to move out of my armchair to watch him!

As many as six different kinds of Owls breed in Britain. The best known is the Tawny Owl, or Brown Owl as he is often called, and this is the chap you hear *to-whit-to-whooing* at night. The odd thing about this familiar country sound is that it is not made by one bird, but two. One owl hoots and his mate answers the call; just which of the two birds do the *'whit'* part and which the *'whoo'* sound I do not know!

The slightly smaller Barn Owl, although fewer in total numbers than the Tawny Owl, is more widespread geographically, breeding in almost every county in the land. Sadly this fine bird has in recent years declined in some places, not only through the modernisation of barns but, much worse, by being poisoned with farm pesticides; these chemicals accumulate in the bodies of mice and voles and eventually make this source of food lethal to the Owls.

The Little Owl, the species which uses our cottage 'phone wires as a hunting look-out, is a dark grey and white streaked bird – a foreigner who has become naturalised since it was first introduced into Northamptonshire from the Continent in the nineteenth century, and from where it spread quite rapidly all over the country. Little Owls are noisy birds, particularly in Spring when the male repeats its note of *cu-cu-cu* with monotonous regularity. He also has a peculiar habit of alternately ducking and then drawing himself up to his full height of nine inches!

You are unlikely to see much of the other Owls – the Short-Eared, which hunts its prey by day, or the Long-Eared Owl, a night bird of the forests; still less the Snowy Owl which is rare outside such places as the Shetlands and whose real name is the Arctic Owl.

You could say that 'an owl is an owl is an owl' because its name is similar in many European languages: in German *Eule*, Dutch *Uil*, Danish *Ugle*, in Swedish *Ugla* and in Latin the word *Ulula* comes from the verb *ulare*, which means to howl.

Talking of Owls, such lovable birds, it is good to hear that, thanks to the RSPCA after a nest of European Hawk-Owls was found in a wall due for demolition, work on a £½m. land reclamation scheme was halted. The Owls were spotted in a 35ft high stone wall on the site of an old iron works at Dowlais, in mid-Glamorgan. The county council and the building contractors stopped work until the fledgelings learned to fly. How nice that some people care so much, particularly since the European Hawk-Owl is a rare visitor from Northern Europe and Asia – chiefly known for its very dashing flight.

Chalkland prize

ANOTHER aspect of the countryside now at its best for the naturalist is chalkland. I have in mind, for this region, that eastern end of the great limestone ridge which starts off in the west as the Cotswolds and comes up through the Chilterns into the southern part of Lincolnshire south of Grantham. Here you will see carpets of Kidney Vetch and Horseshoe Vetch, the low-growing deep pink Thyme, the powder-blue Scabious, various elegant Orchids and the modest little Squinancy Wort – one perhaps you do not know by name yet probably often pass on your walks. The word 'wort' usually refers to a plant with medicinal qualities and so it is with Squinancy Wort (just try saying this out aloud – I think it is a lovely sound, tripping off the tongue with such rhythm!). This plant was formerly used to treat the throat infection called quinsy, a name which itself was variously pronounced 'squinsy' or 'squinancie'. The flowers are quite pretty; white veined with pink, and sweetly scented.

For me, chalkland has one prize above all others – the Pasque Flower (*Anemone pulsatilla*) but it is only very occasionally found, and this on chalk grassland. Because, like the vanishing Cowslip and other wild beauties, its survival is now protected I shall not reveal where I can find the Pasque Flower: as a matter of fact the credit goes to my then child-aged son who, on a family picnic, returned from his wandering about the hillside saying 'Look, pretty flower'. In his hand he held the lovely purple, silky-haired Pasque Flower which has fair claim to being the most exotically beautiful flower of all English wild plants.

Gardeners have propagated *Anemone pulsatilla* as a border plant, but farmers have ploughed up many of its old haunts – I even had to watch this being done by the War Agricultural Committee on the Sussex Downs in the early part of the war when they were showing off the ploughing of grassland by night as part of the home-grown food campaign. In the south of our own part of the country, down Cambridge and Suffolk way, the Pasque Flower has been known as Danes' Blood or Danes' Flower for obvious historical connections with early invaders of the eastern seaboard.

It will never rain roses; when we want to have more roses we must plant more trees.
George Eliot, author of *The Mill on the Floss* (1860)

July

Time for a Rest

SOME COUNTRYMEN insist on calling July the silent month, but I have never understood why. True, many of the wild birds have stopped singing now that the nesting season is over, and yet the fields and hedges are full of the sounds of birds feeding. So, too, are the farm crops full of parties of birds, old and young, excitedly searching for food. It is the same story in our garden just now; any day we can see whole families of Thrushes, Blackbirds, Blue Tits and Pied Wagtails busy foraging. The baby birds hop clumsily from flower beds to lawns, and some of the more daring - unable to reach the bird table - even hang around the door of the cottage in the hope we shall throw them some table scraps.

It seems to me that the adult birds are celebrating their release from the never-ending chores of nesting and rearing their young - chores which kept them aloft on tired wings every minute of the day, maintaining the supply of grubs for the babies. Now, like parents when, at last, the children are off their hands, it is time for a rest. Even the village Sparrows have departed with their young families for the fields, there to enjoy themselves (at the farmer's expense I may say) among crops where the grain is already loose in the ears.

It is much the same with the Blackbirds, Thrushes and various Tits and Finches. Having tried to get at our Red Currants and Strawberries, they are now leaving the garden with their second and even third broods.

Only the wise little Robin stays put, knowing that every time we mow the lawns, or cultivate a section of the vegetable plots, there will be a feast of worms for the taking. But having said all this about the departing birds, I should add that the Cuckoo sometimes goes on singing into July – although usually he stops calling before the end of June.

The farmer always hopes for a warm and dry July and for centuries the weather on ritual saints' days has been taken as an omen of what is in store for us. I suppose the most familiar country saying concerns St Swithin's Day on 15th July. St Swithin was chaplain to a King of the Saxons a thousand years ago, and the rhyme goes like this:

> On St. Swithin's day if thou'll be fair,
> For forty days shall rain nae mair,
> But if St. Swithin's thou be wet,
> For forty days it raineth yet.

On the continent they have a similar piece of folklore but with an earlier date – St John's Day, on the 24th June. In Nature itself, St John's Day is a genuine seasonal changing point, falling as it does three days after the summer solstice – or midsummer. St John has also given his name to the attractive yellow flower called St John's Wort which comes into full bloom in July on hedgebanks, moors and coastal dunes.

Try squeezing the buds of these flowers; you will find they exude a red, oily liquid. And if the heart-shaped leaves are held up to the light they show small glandular needle-like perforations. In fact, the Latin botanical name of St John's Wort is *Hypericum perforatum* and much folklore is woven around the plant's characteristics. The red liquid was regarded as proof that the plant had grown out of the blood of the beheaded John the Baptist and this so angered the Devil that he punctured all the plant's leaves to destroy it! And so it was that the plant came to be regarded in rural England as a talisman against evil. Cattle and horses were even wreathed with St John's Wort to protect them from witches and demons abounding at the time of the summer solstice – hence the French phrase *'avoir toutes les herbes de la St Jean'*, to be ready for anything.

The plant also has a tradition of healing powers, recalled by such names as 'touch and heal' and 'balm of warrior's wounds'. In the thirteenth century a volume called the *Great Life of St Hugh*, the Burgundian Bishop of Lincoln, the story is told of a woman who, after the bishop's prayers and the use of St John's Wort, rid herself of a demon lover and from this account the plant gathered fame as the centuries went by; ballads and tales linked it with other evil lovers and by the sixteenth century Bancker's *Herball* declared 'The vertue of St. John's Wort is thus – if it be putte in a manner house there shall come no wycked spryte therein'.

Harebells

Cure for migraine

JULY flowers – fair, sweet and medicinal was the general verdict of the early botanists. And what a glorious pageant July provides – probably the best wild flower month of the entire year. In this one month over 700 different species are in flower in Britain and, thinking of the descriptions in the early herbals, it is surprising how much use the medieval physicians made of wild flowers. In particular, fascinating traditions are attached to plants called Self-Heal (*Prunella vulgaris*) and Common Dodder (*Cuscuta epithymum*).

For obvious reasons, Self-Heal is also known as Heal-All, or Woundwort. The plant is easily found in hedgerows and around the edges of fields; it has rather thick, square stems only a few inches high and bearing violet-purple flowers. Occasionally it has pink or white flowers and although I have not myself found these variations a doctor-cum-botanist friend has photographed them on the Lincolnshire-Leicestershire borders.

The ease of finding the Self-Heal plant no doubt led to its commonest former use in stemming blood from domestic mishaps – hence such local names as the Carpenter's Herb, Sicklewort, or Touch-and-Heal. The plant contains a volatile oil, an alkaloid, and tannic acid. The Chinese (always great on their herbs) use it for the treatment of gout and urinary problems, whilst our own physicians of the sixteenth century – seeing a resemblance between the shape of flowers of Self-Heal and the human throat – introduced it to help in diseases such as quinsy and diphtheria.

Common Dodder, a parasitic plant is less well known than Self-Heal. In some parts of the country Dodder is known as Red Tangle, or Devil's Thread and it is easy to see why. The stems of Dodder are thin and tangled, crimson in colour and they wind tightly round a host plant, often Nettles, Hops or Wild Thyme. The ancients used to believe that the Devil spun the Dodder at night to destroy Clover and, since Clover was created by God, then Dodder had to be the Devil's weapon! Time was, before the coming of selective weedkillers, when a single stem of Dodder could kill the Clover over an area of thirty square metres. But the apothecaries considered it good stuff, especially for the treatment of what they termed 'obstructions, spleenful headaches and the scabbie evil'.

If you suffer from migraine here is some valuable news: modern medicine is increasingly turning again to some of the centuries' old apothecaries' remedies and the leaves of Feverfew (a wild plant of the Chrysanthemum family having pale green, rather feather-like leaves and attractive little white flowers) are showing excellent results in the treatment of migraine cases which have failed to respond to orthodox drugs.

Leaves of the Feverfew (often called Featherfew) are eaten in bread and butter sandwiches – by the way, adding a little honey or sugar will make them taste less bitter – and as many as 70 per cent of patients in a survey at London's King's College Hospital reported their attacks to be less frequent, less painful – or both, after the Feverfew tests. One third of the sample had no further attacks at all yet had previously shown no improvement or orthodox medicines.

'In the worst headache this herb exceeds whatever else is known'. So, in 1772, wrote Dr John Hill, a Covent Garden apothecary much patronised by the aristocracy. Now, over 200 years later, not only has Feverfew passed modern clinical tests with flying colours but that distinguished London physician and Editor of *The Practitioner*, William A.R. Thomson M.D. (always my tutor, I am proud to say, when he appointed me to launch the journal *Medical News* twenty years or so years ago) is on record as agreeing the value of this wild plant. The only restriction, adds Dr Thomson, is that it should not be taken by pregnant women or children under sixteen. Recommended dose: one large leaf, or three small ones, eaten daily in a sandwich – as described above. And, by the way, you can pot up Feverfew plants and keep them indoors during winter. Out of doors it does best in semi-shade.

Feverfew as an old physic herb, was virtually the aspirin of the Middle Ages – *quasi fugans febres*, 'putting fevers to flight'. Philip Miller, in his *Gardeners Dictionary* of 1741, mentions the plant as being grown commercially for the London market.

Because I am so enthusiastic about the medical and nutritional uses of wild plants I must also tell you about the merits of Comfrey – still flowering this month, although it began in May. Comfrey is a hairy, rather tall perennial with bell-shaped flowers which can be anything from pink, mauve, cream or white and it grows in damp places and beside streams. No good picking if for the striking flowers – they at once shrivel; flowers, leaves, stem – the lot. But it is one of the most useful of all our wild plants, with a higher vitamin content in its leaves even than Spinach (cook it the same way as for Spinach).

A herb-tea, also made from the leaves, was recommended for pleurisy, bronchitis and other chest complaints; and a decoction of the roots is still used as a gargle for pharyngitis and tonsillitis.

Comfrey leaves dipped in batter and fried are a popular dish in Bavaria (see German cookery books under Schwarzwurz) and the leaves, as I said, are a good alternative to Spinach. The famous Gerard, in his *Herbal* of 1633, gives the following sound advice (and a warning!)

> The slimie substance of the roote made in a posset of ale, and given to drinke against the paine in the backe, gotten by any violent motion as wrestling, or overmuch use of women, doth in fower or five daies perfectly cure the same although the involuntarie flowing of the seed in men be gotten thereby.

Flowering right through from July to October, brightening up waste places and railway embankments, is the yellow Snapdragon-like flower called Toadflax (*Linaria vulgaris*). In a few parts of the Midlands it is wrongly called Larkspur, but this is an annual garden species of the graceful and majestic tall perennial Delphiniums hybridised from the wild Delphinium *elatum* of Southern Europe (incidentally, perhaps I may here add that no achievement in half a century of cottage gardening has given me more pleasure than the honour of having a light sky-blue Delphinium named after me, and first displayed at Chelsea just after the war by the world-famed plant raisers Blackmore and Langdon, at Bath).

At the Lakeside

ON A WARM summer day there are few places I like better than to sit beside a quiet, hidden lake to watch Kingfishers and Dragonflies displaying all their brilliant colours. The scene conjures up for me those emotive lines from W.H. Davies' poem *The Kingfisher:*

> *So runs it in my blood to choose*
> *For haunts the lonely pools, and keep*
> *In company with trees that weep.*

Where I go a meadow of permanent grass slopes down to the lake and in July the field is as full of wild flowers as an herbaceous border with garden blooms: great clumps of Purple Loosestrife, Willowherb, Water Dock, the exquisite Flowering Rush with its pink flowers, some Yellow Water Iris and, on the lake itself, white and purple Arrowhead – so called because its floating leaves are shaped like arrows.

Dragonflies are the fastest flying and oldest species of insect in the world. They fly at up to 60 miles an hour, and their fossilised remains show that there were Dragonflies 300 million years ago. Dragonflies, of which there are nearly thirty different species, have a smaller relative called the Damselfly – and this is how to distinguish them: the bigger of the two is the Dragonfly and it rests with its wings straight out beside the body whereas the Damselfly closes its wings above its head like a butterfly.

Blue, green and red, these insects dart over and alongside the water, a magnificent sight indeed. Every now and then you will see two Dragonflies oddly connected and flying in tandem. The male flies in front, holding the female by the neck and this is the first part of mating. During the flight the female Dragonfly curves her body round until the tip of her abdomen touches the male's reproductive organs and collects his sperm. On rare occasions I have, soon after a mating flight, seen the eggs being deposited underneath the leaves of the yellow and white Waterlilies which cover the particular lake I have mentioned.

Only once was my reverie disturbed. Two walkers approached me to ask if I would go and identify what they described as 'a horrible great big insect with a curved sting on its back'. Something foreign they thought it was, and it certainly did look vicious, skulking among rubbish in a hedge-bottom. But the insect was harmless, despite its appearance. It was a Scorpion Fly and what looks like a Scorpion's sting curved over its back is, in fact, the male genitals. These flies scavenge in the hedgerow for dead insects and during the summer they make many short, quick flights in search of food before later on burrowing underground for the winter. Countrymen call them the Devil's Coachman. This is quite descriptive, if you think of the curved piece on its back as being a coachman's whip.

Now a much lovelier thing – the Kingfisher, Britain's most beautiful bird. I get more radio listeners' letters about Kingfishers than any other bird, most of them complaining that the writer has never seen a Kingfisher! For his fishing operations the Kingfisher likes to perch overlooking the water, a hanging Willow branch being a favourite vantage point. Once captured, a fish is carried back to the perch where the bird bangs the fish's head on the tree branch until the fish is dead, or stunned, after which the Kingfisher swallows it *head first*. This way the bird avoids choking on the scales.

Never since, at the age of about ten, seeing my first Kingfisher flash over a stream across the fields around my grandfather's country vicarage near Ashbourne, in Derbyshire, have I ceased to wonder at the iridescent blue of this bird's plumage. No wonder it is claimed to be our most beautiful bird - blue above, with elegant rust-red underparts and a pattern of red, white and blue on the cheeks. Grandfather said that it is a bird only the righteous see!

The exotic colours are intended to warn predators that its flesh has a foul taste - so, too, is a Kingfisher's nest rather foul smelling. Only once did I put my hand down a two-foot long burrow in a sandy river bank to find the white eggs lying in a nest of stinking fish bones. Now I am content just to sit and admire the colours of the Kingfisher as he goes about his business - the pity is that whenever we have a severe winter the numbers of these not very common birds are further reduced.

Canal revival

CANALS throughout the Midlands (even in 'Brummagem' with its more miles of these inland waterways than Venice itself!) are rich in wild life despite the often very inhospitable environment of industrial towns.

Whilst it was to a lifelong canal enthusiast like myself, a sad thought that most of our formerly commercially thriving canals were killed off by the expansion of railways a century ago, more and more sections of disused canals are now being restored for traffic or cared for as Nature Reserves. The best news for some years comes in the 1983 annual report of the British Waterways Board. This reveals not only a surge of trade back to the canals but also that lorry transport is being undercut by as much as £3 a ton on goods carried. Government aid, and lots of keen volunteer help (of the dedicated kind that is achieving so much on preserved steam railways), is making it possible to carry out vital repairs and commercial tonnage on waterways has risen by eleven per cent in a year. The heritage of our canals can, and will, be revitalised to make them the economic and leisuretime asset they should be - to say nothing of reducing the damage at present being done to our roads and historic towns by juggernauts. (It is thanks to the *Daily Telegraph* than I can reproduce overleaf the delightful cartoon from Peterborough's column.)

I can tell you of a well-restored but quiet piece of Midlands' canal well worth visiting for its very striking and lonely scenery. This is the Leicester line of the Grand Union and consists of a short branch going off to the Northamptonshire village of Welford, hard by the site of the Cromwellian battle of Naseby Field in 1645. It is in this countryside that the Grand Union itself reaches a summit level of over 400 feet and crosses over the little Warwickshire Avon on an unseen viaduct.

"Damned Juggernauts"

Yellow and Grey Wagtails love it here and indeed both are among my favourite birds. These Wagtails can be seen on another peaceful stretch of Midlands canal at Cromford in Derbyshire. This canal, first used in 1794 and along which I have this year travelled silently in a horse-drawn narrow-boat, has the recorded sightings of no fewer than 86 species of bird to its credit.

It is not often one sees the Yellow Wagtail since its extrememly slight body is hidden by the lush ferns and other plants that hang gracefully from crevices in the low stone walls. However, I do know one charming spot where the Yellow Wagtail makes himself very conspicuous and this is a rock-strewn beach at the mouth of the Firth of Forth in Scotland glorying in the name of Meikle Poo Craig (sounds like a children's story book place; in fact, translated from the Gaelic, it means 'medium-sized Crab rocks'). From time to time family business nearby takes me to this lonely part of the East Coast and there we can sit and watch anything up to twenty or more Yellow Wagtails flitting about at low tide catching flies for their young – what a lovely reward for going out beachcombing for a bit of driftwood!

Study in lilac

AS WEED CONTROL on farmland has become more and more efficient, many of the wild flowers that once carpeted the meadows have become restricted to road-side verges. These verges have become a refuge for plants like Buttercup, Field Poppies, Corn Marigold and occasionally

Cowslips. Similarly, on the chalky downs, sheep pasture has in many places given way to the ever increasing production of cereals, and flower species such as Cinquefoil and Flax we now see only on the road verges. But even here there is a danger to plant survival from chemical spraying, exhaust fumes and ill-timed council midsummer mowing operations (a good example of this is the loss of Bird's-Foot Trefoil).

Our thanks go to various county naturalist trusts for their efforts to get co-operation from local authorities in maintaining policies which will preserve our wild flower heritage. In some areas more roadside mileage is being set aside as nature reserves and this is excellent news.

Having said this, imagine my delight on recently discovering a glorious patch of pale lilac-coloured flowers, three feet or so tall, on the roadside edge of a copse in Leicestershire. I had of course, to investigate and what an unforgettable sight greeted me when I stopped my 1957 MG (called my barouche hereabouts), got out and pushed my way through a jungle of tall Nettles beneath which lay treacherous pieces of rotting timber in a damp ditch. The flowers looked like small Canterbury Bells, so I knew it was a *Campanula* of some sort. It was obviously paler in colour and had much larger leaves than the wild *Campanula* I knew – the Nettle-leaved Bellflower (or Bats-in-the-Belfry as countrymen call it). For identification purposes I cut a few specimen stems to take home and such was their beauty arranged in an old copper jug, that a botanical artist could hardly resist painting them (and, incidentally, my artist grandmother made much point of the fact that one of the happiest unions of art and science is found in botanical illustration. I agree with her). Anyway, along this High Leicestershire lane I had found the Great Bell-flower (*Campanula Latifolia*), and this is classified as rare except in certain wooded areas of more northern counties.

Apart from its exquisite pale lilac colour, I think perhaps the most distinguishing feature of the Giant Bellflower is that its leaves join the main stem without stalks. A mile further on, there was another and if anything still bigger patch of this lovely flower easily visible to passing motorists but, of course, I am not broadcasting its whereabouts for fear of misguided folk picking the lot (roots and all).

On the subject of conservation, the Dean of Winchester, the Very Rev. Michael Stancliffe, gives me permission to quote these words from an article on God the Gardener: 'The natural world in which Man is set is not a waste nor a jungle but a garden – more strictly an enclosed park, for that is the meaning of the word at the root of the Greek *paradeisos*. The environment in which we live is one of order and fruitfulness and our job is to 'dress it and keep it' (Genesis 2.15) with all the suggestions of conservation and preservation which that verb carries.'

In the early 1930s the Dean's father worked as a parish priest in the Grantham area and was a familiar figure cycling round the villages as a

Diocesan Inspector of Schools. Visiting the school at Welby on June 7th 1931 he noticed an unusual specimen in a bunch of wild flowers – Mr Stancliffe was indeed lucky as the flower some child had brought in was the Lizard Orchid (*Himantoglossum hircinum*) and this rare find was photographed for the *Grantham Journal* on July 11th that year over half a century ago. I have never found this chalk-loving orchid but botanists say it has a goaty smell to its long spike of greyish, purple-green flowers. Sounds lovely! The plant is called the Lizard Orchid because part of the flower looks like the tail-end of a Lizard.

Now come with me in your mind's eye to a dale alongside a tributary of the River Esk on the North Yorkshire Moors. I was there walking one day last July: or rather both walking and enjoying a nostalgic steam trip on that classic piece of industrial history – Stephenson's railway over the moors from Pickering. Again, I am giving away no clues on exact whereabouts, but there beside the fast-flowing little river, bordered as it is by lush woodland and masses of pink Dog Roses, I found two other wild flower treasures new to me. First, there was a tall plant in a boggy piece of land carrying umbrels of white flowers on top of hollow, ribbed stems – and this turned out to be Narrow-leaved Water Parsnip (*Berula erecta*), but in fact it smells more like carrots than parsnips! Officially, this is only *fairly* common in wet areas. But better still was to come before my wife and I walked the last three miles to get the moors railway back to the town in which we had left the car.

A tall-growing bright blue flower caught my eye and at first I thought it was Chicory, lovely enough in itself to be sure – but no! This time it was indeed a rarity (in fact my books say it is *very* rare). I had, it seems, found the Alpine Lettuce (*Cicerbita alpina*). It looks nothing at all like a lettuce, but that matters not; I was very excited, almost jumping for joy – until I realised we had left the camera in the car miles away!

Travelling alone

WHAT a pity it is, towards the end of July, to see so many Hedgehogs squashed to death on the road. The reason so many Hedgehogs do get themselves run over just now is because Mrs Hedgehog, having raised her little family, is busy taking the youngsters with her in search of food.

The Hedgehog is quite a common countryside animal and yet so very few people know much about them. The first Hedgehog lived about 25 million years ago – compared with Man's one million or so years. Today there are nineteen different kinds of Hedgehog and they can be found in Europe and Africa, but oddly enough not in America. Hedgehogs eat small things like insects and so are usually found wherever there are dead leaves and vegetation – in deciduous forests, in damp scrubland and hedgerows and, of course, in our gardens and parks (a Hedgehog in the garden will help keep you free of Slugs). If you go out looking for the Hedgehog then take my advice and go by night because that is when they trot out looking for food; and once a Hedgehog is full up then he sleeps all day! Leave a Hedgehog alone and the spines lie flat, pointing backwards. Disturb the Hedgehog and the first thing he does is to stop moving along and to raise the quills on his head. The more you worry him the more spines are raised. Then, finally, instead of running away from you, the Hedgehog will roll himself into a tight ball knowing there is little you can do about that.

I have studied the anatomy of the Hedgehog and very intriguing it is. The back of the animal is covered with a large sheet of muscle underneath the prickly skin. When the Hedgehog rolls up he tightens this muscle which then makes a kind of bag into which tucks his tail, his legs and his head and so becomes a dangerous ball of spikes. No wonder he has so few enemies. As far as I know, only Polecats, Badgers and Foxes know just how to unroll and eat the Hedgehog, but nobody understands how they do it.

The Hedgehog puts into practice that wise old saying that 'he travels fastest who travels alone'. Apart from the young at breeding time, the Hedgehog lives alone and during the summer it sleeps by day in a nest in a wall and I have found one or two in empty rabbit holes. Come winter and the Hedgehog partially hibernates and in doing so, as a warm-blooded animal, he is unusual: during the winter most mammals stay active and, like humans, keep up their body temperature whatever the weather.

The Hedgehog's secret of survival lies in his being able to convert himself into a cold-blooded creature like reptiles and amphibians, allowing his body temperature to go up and down with that of the air. But there is one snag to this otherwise splendid life-style: it only works when the temperature stays above freezing point – to survive below that the Hedgehog has to use up a store of brown fat to maintain minimum body heat. He is weakened and if, to find food, he comes out of hibernation too often, then he may die.

Out walking one July evening just as it was getting dusk, and having spent quite a time watching the Hedgehog work his way along a dike in search of his supper of slugs, worms and beetles, I was soon rewarded by the sight of a few Bats flying around in the evening sky. I say 'rewarded' because Bats are getting scarce enough to be the subject of care and protection orders. The Bats I saw were, like the Hedgehog, out hunting for food – in their case moths and other flying insects. One of the oddest bits of countryside folklore I ever heard my old grandmother quote concerned guessing a woman's age (and you all know how some ladies try to pull the wool over your eyes on that score!) In Grandma's own words 'If some old *hen* woman tries to fool you she's a *chicken* just forget the illusion she tries to create with her dress and make-up and take her for a walk or drive in the country-side at dusk. If the lady friend is honestly still young and fit she will be able to hear the tiny, high-pitched cries of the Bats but if she is past her best and older then she will be unable to hear a thing.'

As a young man two things struck me about this extraordinary tale: one was that the lovers' evening stroll would need to be near barns or old church towers where Bats were *known* to abound and, secondly, the gentleman would need to know what sound to listen for. Of course, I happen to know! The cries of Bats nesting at dusk sound like *'twink, twink, twink'* and they keep repeating it at regular intervals, but not when they are in flight.

If there are Bats in your loft or outhouses then they enjoy absolute squatters' rights. To harm or remove them could incur a fine of up to £1000 for each specimen, this under the Wildlife and Countryside Act of 1981. By law householders are not allowed to go in for cavity wall insulation, retiling a roof or spray against Woodworm without first obtaining advice from the Nature Conservancy Council (at PO Box 6, Huntingdon) – this is because the chemical used can kill off generations of Bats.

Old railway tracks, like disused canals, are a very rewarding place for the amateur naturalist. Here again I am most fortunate because, near the cottage, is an old single track railway line. This little railway used to carry ironstone from the fields around Belvoir, joining the main line at Bottesford to get to Nottingham and on to the iron and steel making centres of the Midlands. The traffic ceased some years ago – then quite suddenly the line was cleared of the bushes and brambles that had grown over it and we again saw the 30-wagon loads of ironstone going down the line. But all this activity was short-lived; the trains again stopped coming and it was 'back to Nature' on the track once more. But as they say, one man's loss is another's gain and that is certainly true of this forgotten railway.

The best, or perhaps I say most ususual, July event on the old railway was, for me, the finding of a Nightjar's nest on the ground beneath an open patch of Gorse.

The Nightjar is the latest of all our migrant birds to arrive, often as late as the third week in May. Like Swallows, the Nightjar returns to the same spot year after year to rear its young; but where it differs from the Swallow is that the Nightjar (like the Nightingale) travels alone to and from the Mediterranean shores and North Africa. It may sometimes fly with another bird but certainly not in vast flocks, a characteristic which may help Nightjars against the shocking practice in Malta of shooting them in Spring as table delicacies.

This bird is a bit smaller than a Cuckoo, with soft ash-grey plumage and patches of white on its throat. It is rare to see this bird during daytime since it hunts insects by night. The only reason I happened on a nest was because daylight had gone and in the dusk of an early summer evening I heard the unmistakable loud clap which the male Nightjar sometimes makes while in flight. He does this by bringing the wings together very sharply.

Nightjars lay only two eggs in the whole of the season. Very pretty they are, too, being greenish-white, oblong in shape and beautifully veined with brown. The eggs are not even laid in a proper nest – just a spot on the ground where twigs, dead leaves, stones and so on produce an ideal camouflage for eggs and chicks.

Much romance, superstition and – let me admit – utter nonsense has been woven around this uncommon bird of our countryside.

The Nightjar is sometimes called the Night Swallow, or Fern Owl. It has even been labelled, from Roman times and in almost every European country, with the name of Goat-Sucker – the myth being that the bird sucks Goat's milk with the result that the Goat ceases to give milk, becomes blind and dies. This stupid belief led to much persecution of the lovely Nightjar.

The five keys to happiness are to make the most of what God has provided, never to count on anything, not to complain, to choose work that you enjoy and to take exercise.'

(Rabbi) Frank Sundheim

Bridge over the Wye, at Haddon Hall

August

Harvest begins

THIS is the month of holiday-making at home or perhaps by the sea; the month when by the famous 'Twelfth' the wealthy are on the moors to shoot grouse; and the month when the hard-working farmer will be busy with the early part of the cereals harvest.

First of the crops to be cut is Barley. Next come the Oats and finally Wheat. Looking at some of the lovely full-bodied samples of grain on today's farms it is hard to imagine the far-off ancestors of the modern varieties of Wheat. The original wild variety was a thin, bearded thing growing in Central Asia and more like grass than a grain-bearing plant. Through the centuries Man has – by applying Mendel's law of heredity – improved the Wheat plant to its present high-yielding, two or three tons to the acre capacity and the world's farmers have adapted it to every corner of the globe, hot or cold.

At some time or another most people will have heard it said that grains of Wheat recovered from Egyptian tombs of 4,000 years ago and now planted have yielded crops. I do not believe it; there is no evidence to support this claim and I, for one, prefer to believe a well-travelled

Nottinghamshire farmer friend of mine who says wily natives in Egyptian villages keep a supply of fresh corn handy, spreading it when desired to fool the gullible tourist! Much more likely, I think. The fact is that harvested grain does not keep its fertility for years on end. Germination dwindles year by year and vanishes altogether after about fifteen years. Despite this, Wheat kept for a long time does not seem to spoil the flour and bread ultimately made from it; I know personally of a case where some wheat 34 years old was made into excellent bread.

Before the combine harvester went into some Wheat growing near our cottage I took a walk alongside the crop and came across the nest of a Harvest Mouse – the smallest of all our wild animals. They are common enough, but I had not seen a nest for quite some time. The Harvest Mouse is a lovely little thing, measuring little over two inches and having a bright chestnut-coloured coat and white belly. It is because he is such a lightweight and tiny chap that the Harvest Mouse (two of them weigh only the same as a couple of small coins) can move gracefully from stalk to stalk in the Wheat crop. As I watched, I saw the mouse holding on to the straw with his long tail, using it almost like a fifth limb, and sure enough there was his nest beautifully built in the corn and only about eight inches from the ground.

The nest was built of interwoven grass, perfectly round in shape, and when I touched it I was surprised how firm the nest was. I had rather expected it to fall to pieces when I prodded it; but no, it was so hard and compact I could have rolled it like a ball. And I had another surprise coming – inside were eight babies, naked and blind. The minute size of these mice reminded me that years ago a famous naturalist compared the Harvest Mouse with a 12-foot high African elephant and declared that the mouse had practically every separate bone, muscle, blood vessel and other structures present in the massive elephant. The Harvest Mouse is indeed a minute marvel of Nature.

One way and another it was, for me, a very rewarding walk around the field of Wheat – first the Harvest Mouse then, much more of a rarity, a clump of yellow wild flowers called the Corn Marigold. These cheerful looking flowers used to be common enough, particularly on sandy soils, but they were to the cereal grower a troublesome weed. Chemical weed control has solved the problem for the farmer but has, of course, led to the Corn Marigold becoming rare. It grows about a foot tall and has golden-yellow flowers similar to the garden type of Marigold, or Calendula, to give it its proper name. So much was it a feature of the landscape years ago that it influenced place names, supplying the 'gold' part of the Essex village of Goldhanger and the 'gold' of Golding in Shropshire. Anyway, weed or not, I planted a root or two beside our garden hedge to help preserve the Corn Marigold from extinction.

I have, incidentally, had a few requests about ways of helping to preserve our heritage of wild flowers by sowing their seeds. Here is the address from which you can get wild seed – all harvested from our native species: The Seed Exchange, at 44 Albion Road, Sutton, Surrey; supplies can also be bought from Suffolk Herbs, Sawyers Farm, Little Cornard, Sudbury, Suffolk.

Before I left the combine harvesters at work in the Wheat, I picked up a handful of the straw and it set me thinking how beautifully the straw is built up in order that it may support the ears of grain, withstand the wind and rain and convey the nutriment from the soil and air to make the corn. Try splitting open a piece of Wheat straw and see how the separate tubes of which it is made are connected by a little knob, or joint; each 'tube' makes an apex in the lower straw into which the upper one is tongued. The shining material which lines the inside of the ripening straw is silica, deposited there in liquid form to strengthen the tube.

At Haddon Hall

OFF THE FARMS, August is very much the holiday month. In my own case, each year my wife is offered a working holiday at Haddon Hall – thanks to the Duke and Duchess of Rutland whose other home this is besides Belvoir Castle. In this arrangement I am the lucky one, since I too live for a couple of weeks in Haddon Hall – the magnificent medieval manor house near Bakewell, in Derbyshire, and to a naturalist like myself it has an enormous lot to offer (not least, of course, fishing for Trout and Crayfish in the crystal-clear fast running waters of the Derbyshire Wye as it flows beneath the great manor house).

I spend a lot of time not only beside the Wye, and its beautiful tributary the Lathkill, but also wandering around a nearby small, secluded lake. From the Hall to this lake the walk is through an Oak wood and out into a meadow beside the water, the path lined with Forget-me-Not flowers – 'this flower of Heaven's divinest blue' as German poets have described it. There is also a delightful German story which tells of a knight who fell into a fast-flowing river while picking Forget-me-Nots for his lady who was walking beside him. The knight fell into the water and before he was swept away and drowned the gallant gentleman threw the bunch of flowers to his lady, crying *vergisz mein nicht* (forget me not).

Some of the Oak trees in the wood through which I walk are massive specimens. I wonder if you realise what a teeming world of living things just *one* big Oak supports? An Oak tree is, in fact, a fine place to observe the interdependence of animal and plant life. It happens like this – the Oak's leaves, bark, acorns and even roots are eaten or attacked by a variety of animals, many of which are the prey of other animals. As these little creatures die they are broken down by bacteria and returned to the earth, so to nourish it. On average, Oak trees live to about 250 years but they can sometimes go on for several more centuries and each one of these mighty trees can be inhabited by over 200 different kinds of living things – from fungi to insects, birds, animals and parasitic plants.

Another thought always crosses my mind when the woods and surrounding heather-clad moorland in this part of the Peak District are tinder dry in a hot August. The danger of fire is very real after as few as ten days of dry weather – and I recall what a forester once said to me on one of my many childhood visits to Needwood Forest, not far from my grandparents' home: 'from one tree you can make a million matches, but just one match carelessly thrown down is enough to start a fire which will destroy a million trees'. Exaggerated a bit, perhaps, but a dramatic enough warning to visitors.

The early part of August, when I am usually at Haddon, is about the most silent time of the year for birds. The only strong singers seem to be the Yellow Hammers answering each other's calls across the lake and river, but to make up for this out come the Red Admiral butterflies and – at evening fishing time – the Six Spot Burnet moths making for the Thistle heads.

A noble catch

ON ONE OF THESE working holidays at Haddon Hall my wife and I witnessed the weighing of a 5lb Trout caught in the River Lathkill by a member of the Duke of Rutland's family, a young gentleman then aged about fifteen. Naturally enough, much excitement – since it is highly unusual to get a fish as big as that in such a small Derbyshire river.

A handsome fish indeed when you consider that many Trout from similar waters go no more than half a pound or so. The boy's five-pounder was coloured olive and black, with a silver coloured belly; this is typical of Trout caught in *small* rivers, whereas fish taken from big rivers and lakes are all over more silvery.

One of our delightful pastimes at Haddon, and one not needing so much expertise as Trout fishing, is the catching and eating of Crayfish from the stoney banks of the Wye. Crayfish look like small Lobsters and exactly the same thing happens when you cook them – they go bright red (but do not kid yourself that they taste as good!) Crayfish grow to about four inches long and you find them in well-oxygenated, hard-water rivers. Catching the esteemed Crayfish is simplicity itself: no hook, no complicated line and rod; just a short length of stick to which is tied a piece of string with a meat bone on the business end (or, better still, some bacon rind). Once a Crayfish gets the taste of the bait he never lets go and you simply whip him up out of the water into a waiting bucket.

So there we sit on this private stretch of the river bank waiting for Crayfish to come out from their hiding places under stones and burrows on the river side. I know of some Crayfish waters within a short distance of the centres of some of our Lincolnshire towns and I was talking recently with someone who, as a boy half-a-century ago, was able to get an old-fashioned 'tanner a time' – big money then for a lad – selling Crayfish he had caught from the bridge in Avenue Road, Grantham.

'Old Wives' tales

THE ORDINARY coarse fishing on our local, rather sluggish, canal may not have the same elegance as fly-fishing in Derbyshire's fast rivers but make no mistake there is plenty of good sport. In particular, year after year I see some first rate Tench, Roach and Bream pulled out almost every day, except when the weather is too hot. And here, going back to June for a moment, I might add that so keen are the anglers who come from Lincoln, from Nottingham, from Mansfield and from many other parts of the East Midlands to fish this water in the sylvan peace beneath Belvoir Castle that this year the large car park at a local canalside inn was, on the night of June 14th, full up with overnight visitors snatching a little sleep until a minute after midnight when they could officially start fishing on the 15th, the opening day of the season!

A canal fish I mentioned was the Tench, and some very odd folklore surrounds this species. The skin of the Tench contains healing oils and other fish will sometimes be seen rubbing themselves against a Tench when they are sick – hence the origin of the countryman's name for Tench: the Doctor Fish. John Aubrey, a seventeenth century Surrey antiquary and Natural History writer, mentioned what he called 'an approved recipe' for jaundice in which Tench, slit open, were applied to the patient's feet and around his heart. No small wonder that the same Mr Aubrey went on to say that the fish 'will stinke within the hower'. Worse still – the fish had to be left on the patient's body for twelve hours!

Mr Aubrey even advised cutting off the head of the Tench since to look upon it might make the jaundiced patient 'uneasy'. I decided to tell this to one of my canal angler friends since he was eager to show me a fine Tench he had just caught. He gave me the impression, on hearing my tale, that he thought it was *me* who was a bit jaundiced (using this term in the colloquial rather than strictly medical sense).

Around the coast, among people who fish for a living, there are many superstitions concerning fish. For instance, it is believed necessary always to eat Herring and Mackerel from the tail to the head, never the other way lest you turn the heads of the shoal away from shore and so get no more good catches. Another legend has it that Herring shoals are ruled by a leader, a fish above average size and known as a Royal Herring. It is thought unlucky to destroy or harm this fish; if you do so, then the Herring desert that part of the coast.

Bees, referred to several times in this book, are another subject of superstition and folklore and I think one of the strangest beliefs is that Bees are said not to be able to tolerate swearing. If the beekeeper, or a mere onlooker, curses away during hive duties they will most certainly be stung unmercifully. Bees are also said to hate unchastity, or immoral behaviour. They are supposed to be able to sense disloyalty and wrong-doing even when it is undetected in the family of the guilty person and the offender against moral decency and marital loyalty is attacked by numerous Bees! When I was a lad it was believed, in my part of the Midlands, that if a girl could walk unharmed through a swarm of Bees it was a sure sign that she was a virgin.

What is certain is that Bees are extraordinarily *intelligent* insects (even, it is claimed, the most intelligent in the world) and they lead a well-ordered community kind of life. All experienced beekeepers know the value of talking calmly to their stock, so keeping stings away and encouraging the good work of honey gathering. If a Bee comes into your house it is a sign of good luck, or possibly a stranger will be arriving shortly – but you must not kill or drive the Bee away otherwise your luck will be broken; just let it fly away of its own accord.

Month of the blues

EARLIER on I said August was the month of the harvest. Yes, but it is also what I call the 'month of the blues' and by this phrase I mean the colour blue, not depressive moods. It is the 'month of the blues' because blue dominates in wild flowers just now, as did *yellows* in early Spring.

Perhaps the two most striking blue flowers seen along the laneside in August are the Chicory and the Meadow Cranesbill, ancestor of our cultivated garden Geraniums. Knowing something about plant names is always rewarding and in this case the scientific name of Cranesbill is indeed *Geranium*, which is itself derived from a Greek work meaning 'crane' referring to the likeness of the plant's fruit to the beak of the bird called a Crane. So, on your travels, do look out for this most attractive wild flower; it grows about two feet high and has crimson-veined voilet-blue flowers.

Now is the time to find other blue flowers such as Brooklime, with its spikes of dark blue, in ditches and damp places generally: it is a relative of the garden Veronica and its leaves can be eaten in a fresh salad (said to cure scurvy). Another member of the Veronica family is Speedwell, a happy looking little blue flower only a few inches high and plentiful along the roadside verges.

Next in this 'month of the blues' come the Veronica cousins, the Borage family, headed for grand effect by a plant called the Viper's Bugloss. This is a tall plant with rough, hairy stems and its vivid spikes of funnel-shaped flowers are well worth looking out for it you are on the cliffs or sand dunes at the coast. Bugloss is recommended as a cure for melancholy (or should I say 'the blues'). It is called Viper's Bugloss because of the likeness of the plant's spotted, hairy stalk to a viper's skin, and its flower stamens protrude like a snake's tongue.

Perhaps the most appealing and delicate of all the blue flowers of August are the Harebells on hill and moor, nodding their bell-like heads in the breeze that whispers across the valley – and, for me, nowhere more exquisitly sited than beside the Heather and Bilberry-clad hills of the

White Peak, high above the Derbyshire Wye as it passes Haddon Hall to join the mighty Trent en route to the North Sea. Incidentally, the Irish have a charming name for Harebells – they call them Goblin's Thimbles. This is most apt since their pale sky-blue little flowers do indeed resemble the shape of a thimble.

So much for the flowers, but continuing with my blue theme just think of the lovely blue butterflies there are on the wing this month – the Common Blue, the Holly Blue and the Chalk Hill Blue. The first of these, the Common Blue, is plentiful on heaths and open land, even sometimes in the garden too.

All gathered in

BY THE END of the month almost all the harvest is safely gathered in. It is time for Harvest Festival services at church – and yet, somehow, I cannot help thinking about the wild creatures who, all through the growing season, found sanctuary in the standing corn. For such wild life, corn fields were like jungles or forests in which no man walked; forests in which the Rabbits had highways and Mice had safe little bye-ways, their only enemies being Stoats and Weasels.

Once harvest started the wild animals were left with less and ever less cover from their enemies and, by the end of August, I watch them finally scurrying from what is left of their forest seclusion to chance their luck against men with guns, boys with sticks and wildly excited dogs. The countryman knows that Partridges, Pheasants and other birds must be allowed to pass unharmed during the harvesting operations – their fight for survival comes later, when the shooting season opens. But for the Rabbits and Hares harvest time means a deadly gamble against Man.

I suppose to the casual observer it might seem that, apart from more and vastly bigger farm machines, nothing much has changed in the centuries-old scene of bringing in the harvest. But you would be wrong because there are big changes, especially for the naturalist.

For instance, wild flowers that as a boy I often found in corn fields are now rarities. Plants such as the purple Corn Cockle, the yellow Corn Marigold already mentioned, and the blue Cornflower (or Blue Cap to give it the country name) have been sprayed away with insecticides. All that remain common in today's cornfields are the yellow Charlock and Ragwort, pink Persicaria and – despite all chemical control – in certain fields, the red Field Poppy: this survival of the Field Poppy is I think more likely due to weather conditions whereby, in a cold Spring, germination of the Poppy takes place long after the weed killers have lost their effectiveness.

When it comes to the loved-by-all Cornflowers, it may well be that those one does find occasionally are not truly wild but are escapees from gardens. And as for the delicate Corn Cockle, I have not seen them for years and years. The disappearance of Corn Cockle has all taken place within the last 30 or 40 years and I can prove this by quoting from a flower book published just before the last war which cheerfully told us that 'wandering around any cornfield during the summer one is almost sure to find this beautiful flower'. What a pity that is no longer true.

Neither are changes in the harvest fields confined to flowers. Some of the typical birds of the cornfields are also vanishing, none to me more regrettably than the Corncrake (or Landrail). This bird used to be plentiful and its rasping *'creck-creck'* call was a well-loved country sound. But no more. The latest survey puts the number of these birds at only about 650, and nearly all these are in Scotland. The Corncrake's disappearance is largely due to earlier and mechanically faster harvesting giving the birds insufficient time to rear their young before the cover of straw is cut down. I am with those naturalists who suggest that flowers and birds need small uncultivated patches of marginal land and marshes safely out of the way of farm sprays and machines – let us hope at least some farmers will agree.

Haunted cottage

NEAR a five-bar gate entrance to our cottage an Elder tree was encroaching on a small piece of land I had set aside especially for cultivating certain threatened species of wild flowers.

During a casual conversation in the village I was warned by an old man against having the tree cut down lest a witch who lived in the tree would enter the cottage, with dire trouble to follow! And, according to the same source, confirmed by a lady living in a farmhouse nearby, the cottage itself is haunted by the spirit of a little girl who died in it when the house – situated, as it is, well outside the main village in a hamlet of only sixteen inhabitants – was a small nineteenth century isolation hospital (some interesting old-style ribbed medicine bottles have turned up in the garden). Now, they do say, the Victorian child's ghost – we call her Clarice – walks the upper rooms and, indeed, years ago local people wanted nothing to do with the house – far less buy it as I did, complete with Clarice and the Witch in the Elder!

The Elder is a tree steeped in folklore. Other names for it are Bour-tree, in Lincolnshire, and Devil's Wood, in Derbyshire. Certainly, Elder grows like a weed and makes an effective medicine but very poor timber. Elder must not be burnt; if you put it on the fire you will see the Devil sitting on the chimney-pot, or he might even come down the chimney (e.g. in the *Warwickshire Folklore* book of 1911).

Not only did Judas kill himself on an Elder; it was also the tree upon which Christ was nailed. Yet in bark, leaf, cream flower and purple fruit the tones of Elder are most attractive, particularly seen against grey limestone.

Recipes abound in cookery books, but not this one of mine: circlets of blossom (at its best in June) held by the stem, dipped in batter, fried and eaten with sugar. Very fragrant – and an Austrian speciality.

Come September and the branches of Elder are heavy with lustrous blackish-purple juicy berries, excellent for making a tonic and health-giving syrup – most effective for children's coughs and colds when drunk hot. Strain enough Elderberries through muslin to make half a gallon of juice, into which is added the white of an egg, well beaten to a froth. Put the juice in a pan, over a slow heat and when it boils skim the liquid as long as any froth rises. To each pint add 1lb of sugar and again boil slowly until you have a sticky syrup. Bottle when cool, covering the neck of each bottle with paper pricked full of holes (failure to do this might lead to an explosion of syrup – this once happened to bottles of the stuff my wife had stored in a wardrobe, with colourful, but expensive results!)

No matter how beautiful some things are away from home, the water in the home village is always best.

Chinese proverb

September

Season of Mists...

SEPTEMBER, when webs of Queen Anne's lace are draped, like washing on a line, over the hedges; September, when seeds on the Ash trees are filling out ready to spiral, like tiny propellers, down to the ground; September when spikes of Rosebay Willowherb set wasteland on fire with rosy-pink flowers; September, when berries get redder every day, and multi-coloured Asters line the pathways to cottage doors. A twilight month – partly Summer, partly Autumn.

    The first signs of Autumn appear this month, particularly on the farm where the pale yellow stubble is being ploughed in ready for the sowing of seed and the start of Nature's own New Year next month. Just at this moment there is, over the countryside in general, a serene and blessed mood. It is a time when countrymen traditionally resort to bold predictions about the winter weather to come. I can always depend on a villager remarking on the great numbers of berries on the Hawthorn trees, informing me that this is a sign of a hard winter to come. A big crop of berries is, they declare, Nature's way of providing enough food for the wild birds. If you also believe that then I am sorry to disillusion you – but a berry crop is heavy mainly when there were favourable pollination conditions in the Spring: the winter to come can as easily be mild and wet as severe and icy.

Then there are countrymen claiming that they can tell what the winter will be like from how deep Roman (or edible) snails bury themselves for hibernation in crevices or under logs and stones. Others believe that if mice dig deep tunnels then we are in for a hard winter – and even worse things are forecast if ants build their nest moulds very high. The truth is that all these things are merely a reflection of *past* conditions.

A lovely September yields an abundance of wild foods for the kitchen – Mr Keats' 'season of mists and mellow fruitfulness', a poem we all learned about at school. In two of my earlier country books (*101 Wild Plants for the Kitchen* and *Wild Fruits and Nuts* - both published in the E.P. 'Invest in Living' series) I stressed the special satisfaction and delights to be derived from gathering for free the bounty of September hedgerows. Blackberries, Elderberries and Sloe, and perhaps best of all the orange fruits on the Rowan, or Mountain Ash, trees.

'Out, fruit go gather but not in the dew' runs an old country saying. It means you should pick the wild harvest only on a sunny day; that way your fruit will be dry and less likely to go mouldy. It is also wise to collect berries before they are over-ripe – and certainly not after Michaelmas Day when it is said Blackberries belong to the Devil and it is unlucky to pick them!

For as many years as I can remember I, and other members of the family, have in mid-September 'gone Blackberrying' as we term it. How many pounds in weight we collect depends, as do the garden crops, on the season's weather but we aim to pick up to five pounds in an hour in an average year. Apart from traditional uses for Blackberries, as in pies or stewed and served with cream, my wife produces a home-made Blackberry wine that looks and tastes as good as an average Port. It is very simple: place alternate layers of ripe Blackberries and sugar in wide-mouthed jars and allow to stand for three weeks. After that time just strain off the liquid and bottle up, adding a couple of raisins to each bottle. Cork lightly at first then, a little later, more secure. Not only is this Blackberry wine so ridiculously cheap to make, but it keeps in fine condition for at least a year.

Wine apart, I have over the years, and from various sources, picked up some very odd bits of information about Blackberries. For instance, the fruit used to be collected by country people and sold to make dyes; in fact, Navy blue and indigo were originally Blackberry juice, and it was also used to dye woollen stockings black. I have seen seventeenth and eighteenth century references to housemaids wearing 'pale lavender ribbons' and this delicate tint was obtained from the humble Blackberry dye.

Butterfly colours

THERE IS AN additional bonus to going out for Blackberries and this is the sight of so many butterflies, attracted by the ripe berries. Their chief appeal seems to be for such butterflies as the Comma, Speckled Wood and, of course, Red Admirals – all of whom can suck up the Blackberry juice with their long, hollow tongues. It is for the same reason that the Red Admirals alight on Plum trees in the cottage garden, sucking the over-ripe windfalls and I am always delighted to see them. The red, white and black colouring of a Red Admiral butterfly is, I think, magnificent and on this score I learned that this butterfly used to be called the Red *Admirable* (deservedly so, I would say!).

Have you ever wondered just what makes the beautiful colours and patterns on butterfly wings? Hold a butterfly in your fingers and the 'dust' from it is, in fact, the minute scales from its wings. Under a microscope you would see that each of these scales is shaped like a flattened bag with a short stalk fitting into a socket in the wing membrane. The scales are arranged like slates on a roof and it is these scales which give the different kinds of butterfly and moth their varying colours and patterns. Some of the scales are filled with coloured pigments – like the scarlet bands on the wings of the Red Admiral, or the 'eyes' on the Peacock. Still other scales on butterflies' wings are grooved and ridged to produce the effect of colour by reflection. One of Nature's wonders, I think, and what harmless, lovely and silent things butterflies are, to be sure.

In Europe alone there are nearly 400 different kinds of butterflies, seventy of which we regularly have here in Britain. These seventy home species are grouped into just seven families and most of the varieties (including the favourite Red Admiral) belong to the family called Nymphalidae or – to use the popular name – brush footed butterflies on account of their most distinctive characteristic, short, brush-like legs.

With so much man-made ugliness around us, I say thank God for butterflies. The pity is that the life of some highly-coloured butterflies is as short as ten days; so do make a point of enjoying *today's* butterflies while you may; some will have gone for ever by *tomorrow*.

We all know that some birds migrate to avoid the worst of the year's weather – and so do butterflies. Unlike the birds, the butterflies fly only a few feet up in the air, unless they run into rising currents of warm air, or thermals as they are called. This way, by merely keeping airborne, butterflies can be carried hundreds of miles. In 1940 I was staying with a friend in Hertfordshire when a horde of Large Whites, covering an area 100 metres wide, took several minutes to cross a cricket pitch, forcing the players to interrupt the game!

Vanishing countryside

ONE of the most outspoken comments I have ever read on the subject of our vanishing countryside sights and sounds was made in a letter to the *Daily Telegraph* by Miss I.E. Pimblett, of Storrington, a village in the South Downs behind Worthing, and what she said about her own district of West Sussex is worth quoting here:

> There used to be an annual migration of Frogs to the pond on a farm, but not any more; the pond has been filled in.
>
> The sound of Lapwings returning to the pastures to nest can no longer be heard as there are no cows to graze the pastures which now grow corn. If the sound of the Lapwings has gone there is, however, a much less joyous sound – that of calves living their brief lives in purpose-built ugly sheds and never leaving them until the day they are transported to France or Italy.
>
> The Swallows were a delight around the farm buildings. They don't come any more; the farm buildings have been reconstructed and there is no easy place for them to build nests.
>
> There was a field with a bank covered with Primroses in the spring. One or two plants survive: the rest have either been sprayed out of existence or ploughed into the ground.
>
> The hedges, white in May with Hawthorn flowers and thick with Blackberries in the autumn, are no longer there.
>
> There was a small wood on the side of the Downs. The farmer has cut it down.

To be quite fair, there is another side to this coin: the area of woodland on farms has gone up by over 218,000 acres in just ten years, reports the

National Farmers Union. Neither is it all conifer forestation; the amount of broadleaved woodland has not fallen and our native Oaks still predominate. Good news indeed – and more to come: a survey by the Country Landowners' Association shows that about three quarters of members have done some amenity tree planting in the past few years – and this means hundreds of thousands of new young trees growing in mixed woods or shelter belts.

On one Midlands estate alone – the Duke of Rutland's 14,500 acres at Belvoir – over 12,000 trees a year are being planted, some to replace specimens killed by Dutch Elm disease; and the Spring Gardens, originally laid out in the early 1800s but abandoned prior to the last war, have been restored by the Duchess of Rutland over the past fifteen years. Here many new young trees, quite apart from plants, are going in every year to add to the splendour that is Belvoir, now and for generations yet to come. Such dedication is what conservation is all about.

Preserving wildlife is no longer just a cosmetic operation. Increasingly, the subject is part of the syllabus at agricultural colleges and, to match this, there is a new mood of collaboration between farmers and those concerned with ways of keeping rural Britain beautiful. It is now obvious to all that planning controls, which have already ruined some historical towns and cities, are no recipe for preserving the countryside – the farmer who is reproached for what he has done is entitled to a wry smile when he sees what builders and planners did after the war to cities like Birmingham and Newcastle. Give farmers the opportunity and I am sure they will be on the side of those who care for the countryside.

One's awareness of the interdependence of Man and Nature, of the formative power of landscape, trees and flowers on the spirit, is at all times of the year very apparent at Belvoir. The poet George Crabbe (1754-1832), who spent some time as chaplain to the Duke of Rutland's household, wrote:

> The walks are ever pleasant; every scene
> Is rich in beauty, lively or serene;
> Rich is that varied view with woods around,
> Seen from the seat, within the shrubb'ry bound;
> Where shines the distant lake...

Nevertheless, I feel there was a touch of irony in Crabbe's writings; he was unhappy at Belvoir, a parson of humble origin ill at ease in a nobleman's home, tormented by the domestics who made him drink glasses of salt water because Crabbe would not join in their Tory toasts. This same Mr Crabbe once borrowed a £5 note and some MSS to seek fame and fortune in Fleet Street – alas, he was by no means the first or the last to have been disillusioned in the Street of Ink!

As he did of Belvoir, the reverend gentleman could have said much the same about the vistas around Grimsthorpe Castle, near Bourne in Lincolnshire. Here is the home of the Willoughby family, one of the few English peerages which can descend through the female line, hence the present Baroness Willoughby succeeding to the title on the death early in 1983 of her father, the Earl of Ancaster. Grimsthorpe provides another epic canvas of English countryside with a distant view of a 'Capability' Brown lake such as Crabbe says *shines* amid trees: a delight to artist and naturalist alike, just as the collection of shrub roses and other plants in the Grimsthorpe gardens are to me, a country cottage gardener. Knowing, as I now do, that years ago a few of the rarer plants here came from the nearby Rectory gardens brings to mind once again what a debt we owe to former generations of English country parsons who so often proved themselves superb plantsmen and hybridists – S. Reynolds Hole, a Dean of Rochester, to name but one in this tradition and whose *Book About Roses* has remained a classic since publication in 1901.

No one denies the material need for maximum home food production and, indeed, the British farming industry's performance has been one of the few bright spots in the early 1980s economic recession. But our landscape heritage of trees and flowers, birds and animals, ponds and hedges is of major concern to us all, farmers included, and a right balance must be kept between conflicting ideals.

The Large Blue

MODERN Modern agricultural methods certainly cannot be blamed for the almost total disappearance of the rare and very beautiful Large Blue butterfly.

This particular butterfly was not only lovely to look at but it was unique in that it depended for food on the Wild Thyme plant and a special sort of Ant. What happened was that the Ants more or less 'kidnapped' the Large Blue butterfly eggs and dragged them to their nests. There the Ants fed on the larvae who, in return, secreted a sort of milk which the Ants enjoyed. When the caterpillars hatched out they ceased to have any value to the Ants and remained underground all through the winter until the Large Blue butterflies emerged the next Spring.

Part of the blame for the disappearance of the Large Blue is said by the Nature Conservancy Council to be due to the loss of Rabbits through myxomatosis – when Rabbits were healthy and plentiful they created the finely-cropped, short grass needed by the butterflies. But we can take heart to some extent – some of these butterflies from Europe are now in captivity at British butterfly farms and it may just be possible to reintroduce the species if a suitable habitat can be found. Odd as it may seem, there are some naturalists who are against the idea of giving

Nature a helping hand in this way, but why I do not know.

The last time I saw Large Blue butterflies was in Devon about four years ago, but for some strange reason that particular summer this small colony of butterflies produced only infertile eggs. Let us hope they have better luck with a colony in south-west Scotland which is being studied by the British Wildlife Society as part of 29 butterfly conservation projects.

As far as birds are concerned, there is a happier side to the story of decline. We may indeed have lost most of our Corncrakes, Woodlarks and Kentish Plovers (to name but a few) but against this there are, in total, more different kinds of birds now breeding in Britain than at the beginning of this century. Hard to believe, but true.

I wonder if weather changes have anything to do with it? It is thought possible that drier, easterly winds since 1950 have enabled birds from northern Europe to spread. Birds of the tundra and forests of Scandinavia are now seen more often and some, such as the Lapland Bunting and Purple Sandpiper, have nested here.

How often, if September weather is good, plants and trees seem to have a second lease of life and come into flower again as though it were April or May all over again. In the cottage orchard as late as the third week in September, a 40 foot high Pear tree has bloomed on some of its outer tip branches. In the garden borders, Polyanthus flowers again and, even more startling, Magnolia and Rhododendron have in some years given us an encore. It can be the same story in the hedgerow along the canalside – plenty of Ragged Robin and White Dead Nettles just now, although their normal flowering time is May and June. Honeysuckle and Ivy also often break the rules – I have picked flowers from a Honeysuckle plant bearing both unripe green berries and ripe red ones, all at the same time; and when most things are dying back for the winter Ivy bursts confidently into small green five-petalled flowers. This is good for insects whose food is now running a bit scarce, and all manner of flying things visit the Ivy for their share of the nectar. In turn, this makes Spiders very happy trapping the insects in those webs that glisten on the hedges this month.

I know not everyone likes Spiders, but I *do* and it upsets me quite a bit to see thoughtless people kill these gentle, useful creatures – after all, spiders have as much right to live as we have. Spiders belong to one of the oldest species of insect on earth, with a history of 350 million years. Their scientific name is the *Arachne* class, named after the mythological maiden of that name. She it was who challenged Athena (patron goddess of Athens) to a weaving contest and was promptly changed into a Spider. That is why it is said to be unlucky to kill a Spider.

In my opinion, Spiders are lovely creatures; from the tiny so-called Money Spider that occasionally rushes over your hand to the big, handsome specimens. The only exception I make is in the case of the

Tarantula, a venomous hairy creature from Southern Europe whose bite was supposed to produce trantism, an epidemic dancing mania. I once saw a Tarantula nearly as big as my fist jump out of a newly-imported crate of bananas in London's old Covent Garden market and watched incredulous as a policeman popped it into a cardboard box!

Spiders spin their webs on warm mornings following a cool night and in these conditions they are often carried aloft by the ascending air currents. It is by this means that Spiders reach the seemingly inaccessible places in which we find them. I have heard it said that when Spiders spin long lines of web thread it means eight or ten days of fine weather; if only short lines are spun, then look out for rain and wind. I have never put this bit of folklore to the test – but, then, neither can I prove true or false the theory that Spiders are attracted by music!

People who kill Spiders as 'useless, nasty creeping things' usually act similarly with Wasps. I am often asked 'what good do Wasps do?' but, of course, both Spiders and Wasps have their uses, chiefly in disposing of disease-carrying flies and, in the case of the Wasp, destroying huge quantities of insect pests harmful on the farm and in the garden. Both insects are also very interesting little creatures if you will take the trouble to learn a bit about them. Wasps, for instance, include both a solitary species and a socially orientated kind which prefers community living and working; it is these *social* Wasps that can be a bit of a nuisance around the house just now when the orchard fruit is ripe and there is honey for tea.

One of the very odd things about these social Wasps is that they include among their numbers both what is called the Common Wasp and the German Wasp. How to tell the difference? Just look straight at the front of the Wasp that is bothering you and if it has an anchor-shaped mark on its face then it is a Common, or English, Wasp; but if the Wasp has three black dots on its face then you can be sure it is German!

Wasps are not inherently aggressive insects and will not normally sting unless you provoke them. In fact, you are more likely to be stung if you wave your arms about trying to get rid of the Wasp than if you ignore it – that way the Wasp will ignore you too.

Purple hills

OF ALL the beautiful things to see in September, for me Heather is among the most colourful and appealing. Or it is because I so much enjoy walking on lonely moorland? (Another of my very own country quirks is shuffling among deep drifts of fallen autumn leaves – I seem to remember an Edith Sitwell poem called *Walking Through Leaves* describing just this delightful feeling.) Anyway, a favourite high moorland tract is at Holymoorside above Chesterfield, and, apart from the Heather and varieties of wild birds I do not normally see, a farmer friend on the moors allows my wife to take her beehives there for the making of Heather honey, among the best flavoured of all.

Moorland is a very individual and varying part of the British Isles landscape and no two moors are the same. Take, for instance, Bodmin Moor in Cornwall; many years ago I spent an entire three weeks walking and sleeping out on this moor when it was still a wild place few people ever visited and certainly its ecology was entirely different from our nearby Derbyshire moors – the reason being, of course, mainly because birds, plants and animals vary according to geographic area and climate.

Ling covers the hillsides high up in Derbyshire. With it you will find the larger-flowered Bell Heather and, where the ground is wet, the pink Cross-Leaved Heath, so named because each group of four leaves is shaped like a cross. Devil's-Bit Scabious and Stonetop are two other nice wild flowers of the hills.

The birds up at Holymoorside include plenty of Linnets, Yellow Hammers and the Twite – sometimes called the Mountain Linnet and which, when cold weather comes, descend to the sea-shore spreading themselves out along the entire Lincolnshire coastline and elsewhere. However, the bird that pleases me most on any of the Derbyshire moors is the Whinchat. Unlike its cousin the resident Stonechat, the Whinchat is a migratory species so perhaps those I see are just 'passing through'. It is a most appealing little brown bird with a plum-coloured breast, and I particularly like the way Whinchats perch very upright on a stone or post before suddenly taking off to flutter around in the Heather, Gorse and Bilberry bushes. Also, just occasionally the greater Spotted Woodpecker can be seen tapping on some small hillside Oak.

I have spent many happy hours not only on moorland but also lying lazily on the chalk downlands of Kent and Sussex more or less just for the sake of watching another favourite of mine – the Wheatear. These jaunty grey, white and orange feathered birds of the open countryside fascinate me, flitting from one stoney outcrop to another and jerking their white tails whilst uttering a sharp *'chack-chack'* sound.

My visits to the Derbyshire moors are not entirely devoted to watching wild birds. A prime object is also to pick Bilberries to make a Bilberry Tart, considered by many connoisseurs to be the best of all fruit tarts. You make Bilberry Tart as you would any other fruit tart, but as the very juicy blue-black coloured Bilberries reduce down so much the secret is to put the white fluff of baked apples *under* the Bilberries in the dish, so sopping up the juice and giving your tart more body. And the final touch of epicurean delight comes from putting just a few leaves of Mint here and there on top of the Bilberry layer. Yet another delightful taste is that of wild Raspberries growing at a few spots in the hills above Bakewell – somehow quite different from the flavour of cultivated Raspberries.

It is not until September that, back at home, I become fully aware of a few Green Woodpeckers regularly working the Oaks and Elms over on what we call 'the pastures'. This month the sounds are jubilant and they come from *young* birds, easily identified as such by their immature mottled plumage and lack of the adults' crimson-coloured head crests.

Greater Spotted Woodpecker

Through field glasses I have watched the youngsters playing pranks on each other – one bird flits to an Oak and rattles noisily in the highest branches. Then a second young Woodpecker glides in after him to flutter on the lower branches and scream his head off until yet another bird arrives to chase the first two! Call it Hide-and-Seek if you like; it is certainly all very odd and ornithologists say it is training for the vigilance that, more than most birds, the Green Woodpecker needs to survive such woodland hazards as hawks whose attention is drawn to the Woodpeckers by the tree tapping noise made in their search for insects.

Willie o' Douglas Dale

ALTHOUGH I am not keen myself, many people just now seem to be busy making wine of one kind or another (beer as well, come to that, but you could hardly call me an enthusiast for this either. I agree with Dr Johnson in believing an inn is the only right place to drink beer). That said, I have no wish to knock the home-made wine hobby if you enjoy it; in fact, my wife is keen and certainly the most attractive looking wine she makes comes from this month's Rowan, or Mountain Ash, berries and made according to an old Midlands recipe. This wine starts off as a cloudy pinkish liquor but after fermentation it becomes a clear and deep shell pink; such a lovely colour that it almost tempts me to drink it.

The mere sight of this wine sets me off thinking about the Mountain Ash tree and all the legends I have heard about it in my country travels, and these have at one time or another taken me into every single county in Britain (surprisingly few people seem to know that Britain means only England and Wales. Add Scotland and it becomes Great Britain. Add Northern Ireland and it becomes the United Kingdom.) Rowan is a Scandinavian name for the Mountain Ash and is the name commonly used in the Midlands; in the south it is called Quickbeam or Whitty.

I rather like a nineteenth century Scottish ballad called *Willie o' Douglas Dale* and it told of the character Willie going off to the quiet woods with the King's pregnant daughter and this girl – wishing to ward off the imminent dangers of childbirth – saying:

> O had I a bunch of yon red rodding
> That grows in yonder wood
> And a drink of water clear
> I think it would do me good.

I need hardly tell you that that bit of wishful thinking was 'all my eye and Betty Martin'; but even so it is no stranger than many of the other beliefs attached to the Rowan (or Rodding as the King's daughter called it). In parts of the North Midlands, May the Second used to be called Rowan Tree Witch Day when branches were hung on house doors to ward off evil spirits. In the West Country people believed that if they kept a sprig of Rowan in their pockets they would never suffer from rheumatism, since the complaint was induced by elves and pixies. But it is with good reason that the Rowan is also called the Fowler's Service Tree, this because the berries are an excellent bait for trapping birds. And in the garden this tree, with its orange-red berries is a favourite with Thrushes and Blackbirds.

If you would like to make use of Rowan berries then I would advise you to pick them from now until the end of October, before they become mushy. And apart from the wine I mentioned earlier on, Rowan berries make a lovely sharp-flavoured jelly, delicious with game or lamb. If you happen to come by a Grouse then do try this jelly with the bird – like whisky, it is a matter of tradition!

And so into October, the start of Nature's own New Year and all that it promises us – if we care enough.

Publishing a volume of poetry today is like dropping a rose-petal down the Grand Canyon and waiting for the echo.
Don Marquis, in his column *The Sun Dial*, 1920

October

Nature's New Year

OCTOBER is a prince of months in the countryside, a flamboyant month; a month of transition from summer into autumn with its falling leaves and shorter days.

In this evening of the year there are often clear blue skies by day, streaks of rose madder and turquoise at sunset and at night the hunter's moon hangs like a big lantern from the outer world. Occasional strong winds remind us that we have to say goodbye to summer and welcome the coming winter with all the different pleasures that has in store for the contented man (for me, two of these innocent pleasures are eating hot buttered toast prepared in front of the log fire whilst a strong nor'easter howls over the rooftops; or well wrapped-up, walking in gently falling snow).

My thoughts about October have in no way whatsoever changed since I first set them out one Sunday evening, just a year after war ended, in a BBC Home Service broadcast from London. For being able to reproduce a small part of what I then said I have to thank *The Listener* for publishing my piece called 'Autumn', at that time:

Most years by now the pageant of flowers and fruit is nearly over; high winds often complete what the frost did the night before and cause red and golden-brown leaves to swirl and eddy through gardens and fields and woods... Autumn is a period of living rest, not the silence of death and decay. A grain of Wheat is sown in soil, and while maturing, there it remains for perhaps as long as ten months, on through the Autumn, through the Winter, Spring and Summer. The wise gardener, too, sows many of his seeds now, taking as his example the natural fall to the earth of ripened seed from the parent plants... the seed may germinate quickly into little plants that attain a certain amount of growth and then begin their living rest until Winter has passed; or some may remain dormant in the soil, but essentially alive. October is the month when farmer and gardener proclaim their faith in the order of the universe and in the power that makes things grow.

'It is a time when I stand still and look at the rose beds, their glory almost gone; I look at the flower borders with a feeling of gratitude for their contribution to the beautiful things of this earth...standing like this at the beginning of Nature's rest I am conscious both of the fall of sap in my trees and plants and yet confident that all this will wake up again, with the life that is in it ready - if only I play my part - to give abundantly and to go on giving. It is part of the changelessness of the seasons and that is something which humbles, even conquers, us; says the Book of Genesis (8:22) 'While the earth remaineth, seed time and harvest, and cold and heat, and Summer and Winter, and day and night shall not cease'.

Visually, the chief glory of the month is the wonderful colour of many trees, their berries as well as their leaves turning from green to a whole range of yellows, reds, and browns. And these colours are often matched by those of the evening sky, particularly by what is called a 'Mackerel sky' when the patterns of very high white clouds against a pink background resemble the markings on the sea fish of that name. According to Gilbert White, the eighteenth century naturalist of Selborne fame, these whisps of fleecy cloud often form a triangle over an area of land the shortest side of which is about 50 miles - so quite a lot of people can see the gorgeous spectacle of a 'Mackerel sky' at any one time. What a nice thought and one which I am sure would have been echoed a century later than Gilbert White's time by that other eminent naturalist Richard Jefferies (whose books I have read and re-read since I was at school and to whose life and work I devoted a degree thesis). *'Colour'*, said Jefferies, *'is a kind of food...a drop of wine for the spirit.'*

The Goose Fair

MICHAELMAS DAY itself falls in the previous month, just a couple of days before October comes in, but the whole Michaelmas period is a significant time in the country calendar.

Traditional food for the festival is Goose and the symbolic flower the mauve Michaelmas Daisy. The word Michaelmas comes from the church festival of St Michael and All Angels, the oldest of the 'angel' occasions, and St Michael is regarded as both the protector against evil and the guide to Heaven. Folklore has it that one may sleep late on St Michael's Day and the required hours of sleep were laid down in this old rhyme (with which, incidentally, I totally agree!)

> *Nature requires five,*
> *Custom gives seven;*
> *Laziness takes nine,*
> *And Michaelmas eleven.*

In the East Midlands – an area of England where, last year, tourist spending *rose* by eight per cent compared with a national *drop* of two per cent – one of the happiest events in 'our country year' is the Nottingham Goose Fair. Villagers from the surrounding counties have for generations looked forward to this trip to the big city and joining their town cousins in all the fun of the fair at this, the biggest occasion of its kind in Britain.

We may no longer see hundreds of Geese being driven from Lincolnshire and Norfolk to be sold at the Fair but it has nevertheless remained, throughout its glorious 600 years' history, an exciting and impressive event. Until just over fifty years ago, when the Fair moved to the open spaces outside the city centre, Nottingham Goose Fair was traditionally held in the Old Market Square beneath which, incidentally, my wine-importer great-great-grandfather stored his stock-in-trade in the labyrinth of vaulted cellars. This was the time when the mill-owner brother of that ancestor of mine could refer in a family diary kept in the D.H. Lawrence country at Giltbrook Hall, near Eastwood, to riding over to visit friends at such 'pretty places as Heanor and Bulwell where my daughters admired the cottagers' gardens gay with flowers'. Well, well... they would certainly have a job to pick a nosegay of scented flowers around there now, let alone 'mounting our horses and riding home through the fields in time for tea'. The house, first occupied by my ancestors in 1774, was demolished in the 1960s to make way for an industrial estate.

Back to the sunshine

IT IS IN October we see the last of the Swallows leaving to winter in Africa. Departure dates of both Swallows and House Martins are flexible and just before I get up in the early mornings I always first glance out of the bedroom windows to see whether any of these familiar and likeable birds are still flying around. I have seen the odd Swallow or House Martin as late as November (a matter I refer to again in the following chapter).

I do not think any one really knows just what determines bird departure dates and I often wonder, watching Swallows chattering away in groups on the telephone wires, whether they are debating their flight schedules!

Migration is, and always has been, one of the great mysteries of Nature. What we do know is that most migrating birds depend for their food on creatures which hibernate or else lie beneath the frozen ground in winter. Once the readily available food supply disappears, off go the birds. The age-old question is, of course, how do they find their way back to Africa or wherever? And, come to that, how does a Swallow or Swift arrive back here again the following Spring to the exact nesting spot in the farm outbuildings where it was born? The current extensive marking of birds with identification rings, and scientific aids such as radar, are producing data which might eventually solve the migration mystery but, until then, all we can assume is that day flying birds navigate by the sun; night fliers by the stars. And, try as you will, you cannot beat the birds' instinct – for instance, in one test of navigational skill a Manx Shearwater (a bird rather like a Puffin) was taken to Boston in America and from there it found its way back over 3000 miles of featureless ocean to its nest on Skokholm Island, off the South Wales coast.

We know that animals and birds migrate to feed and breed – and yet there seems no physical reason why, for instance, the Arctic Tern should fly 11,000 miles from Britain each year to winter in the frozen Antarctic; or why the lovely Painted Lady butterfly should leave Africa and come to England where neither it, nor its offspring, can survive our winter.

Migration traffic is not, of course, all one way. We have our own winter tourist trade. Birds like Fieldfares and Redwings, both relations of the common Thrush, will be arriving here this month and we shall hear that lovely call of the Redwing as they feed on berries along the canalside. Their call is as clear as a note sounded on a flute; something like *Trui... Trui...Trui.* And soon we shall have the pleasure of seeing visiting water birds – the Barnacle Geese from Spitzbergen, White-Fronted Geese from Siberia and Pink-Footed Geese from Iceland.

A breakfast treat

IN EXTOLLING the joys of October I make no excuse for returning to the subject of autumn colours of trees and hedgerows. Half way through the month the Horse Chestnut and Limes, and other trees, are splashed with yellows and crimson, just at the Hawthorn and Wild Rose bushes are loaded with scarlet berries.

Even on the stillest day the coloured leaves fall to the ground. At the base of each leaf stalk is a special group of cells known as the layer of separation and as the season advances this layer becomes dry and corky. Finally, the attachment of the leaf stalk is so weak that the leaf flutters to the ground by its own weight. Wind or frost help bring down the coloured autumnal leaves but they are not, as most people think, the cause of leaf fall. (How apt is the American term 'the fall', meaning autumn).

On my walks to enjoy the autumn colours, I try to combine two other of my favourite country pastimes – and one is Mushroom picking. First, there is the pleasure of an early morning walk through the dew-soaked meadows and then, to follow, fresh mushrooms served with the breakfast bacon! And this is, of course, a good month to find all sorts of edible fungi besides Mushrooms. Very few of our native fungi are poisonous; most are good to eat even if some varieties are what is called 'an acquired taste'. But even so, do be careful. Two sorts to avoid are the Fly Agaric, which is scarlet with white spots, and – this one rather more difficult to identify – the Death Cap with its olive-green top and pure white gills. However, a good fungus you *can* eat is the Orange Peel, so named because on bare ground in the autumn woods it really does look like orange peel. Another is the Witch's Butter, common enough on dead Oak tree branches; other lovely names for this are Candle Snuff, King Alfred's Cakes and Shaggy Ink Cap.

My second pleasure on October morning walks, especially when I cannot find any Mushrooms, comes from picking a pound or so of Sloe fruits to make Sloe Gin for Christmas. The Sloe (or Blackthorn) is the sourest berry you will ever taste and is the ancestor of all our delicious cultivated plums. Mid-October onwards is the best time to pick these bluish-black coloured berries, particularly after the first good frost as this makes the tight skins of Sloe berries softer and more permeable. Some authorities have said that certain types of so-called Port wine began with the skins of British Sloes rather than the grapes of Portugal.

Be that as it may, if you go out in October and pick yourself a pound of Sloes, the gin made from them will be just right for drinking at Christmas. It is all so very simple. Put your Sloe berries into a large fruit-bottling jar and fill with gin. Cork securely and store in a warm but dark cupboard. Just before Christmas the Sloe Gin, of a lovely pink colour and having a unique piquant flavour, should be poured into bottles. It is then ready for drinking but it can stand rather longer with ultimate advantage in flavour.

Where are the Otters?

OTTERS are high on the list of endangered species, fast disappearing through river pollution, hunting and trapping by water bailiffs working on Trout and Salmon rivers.

Certainly in the Midlands, the charming and playful Otter has retreated from our lowland rivers during the past thirty or so years and much understandable excitement was caused in 1982 when a few were seen on the Lincolnshire-Nottinghamshire borders. I have not myself seen an Otter these past ten years, not even in the moorlands and hill rivers of Derbyshire and further north, yet time was when they were in most of Lincolnshire's river systems, including the Witham and the Bain.

Regretfully, I do not think the recent sightings mean the Otter is on his way back to us; rather that these few that have been seen have strayed south from rivers on the Derbyshire and Yorkshire moors in search of food: not at all unlikely since Otters can and do travel great distances overland.

I am not giving up my own search for Otters and have taken the advice of the Lincolnshire Naturalists' Union, giving in a useful little booklet called *Where to Look for Mammals, Amphibians and Reptiles in Lincolnshire and South Humberside*. Yes, comprehensive it certainly sounds, and comprehensive it is. But for me, no luck so far despite – as the booklet told me to do – first looking for partly-eaten fish and eels, fish scales, webbed tracks and the Otter's most distinctive droppings (or spraints, to use the correct term) left at carefully selected places to act as a warning to other Otters that 'this is my territory – please keep off'!

The tell-tale signs of Otters I looked for as a boy were their slides down river banks into the water. Otters love to play, and thoroughly enjoy sliding down troughs of mud, or even snow, into a river. Or, when my cousin and I dared to leave my aunt's farm at night, she and I would listen for the Otter's whistle and we were rarely disappointed. But no longer. Nowadays I could spend all night beside the same Warwickshire river and not an Otter's whistle to be heard.

Should you be lucky enough to see an Otter at the present time, do please tell the Nature Conservancy Council who are doing valuable work trying to restore the Otter population. One idea being tried is to release captive-bred stock so, who knows, the day may come when we might again see on a summer's evening that lovely break in the surface of some quiet river pool and hear the low whistle of the Otter, as if to say 'I'm back!'

Come into my parlour...

I HAVE been watching Spiders again, or rather their webs along the garden hedge and draped all over a round Box shrub just outside our bathroom window.

Early one morning the sun was shining through the webs, glistening on the dew-soaked silks, and what intrigued me was the fact that each web had a female Spider in the centre and on the outskirts of the webs, where the silken lines ran down to a nearby low wooden flower tub, were male Spiders. As I watched I could see that these patient male suitors, although keeping their distance, were obviously trying hard to impress the females in this peak mating season for Spiders.

On one web were three amorous males all after the same lady's favours. But too bad; she seemed to be ignoring them all, with the result that two of these frustrated chaps resorted for sport to attacking each other! Mind you, there was some good thinking going on; the third Spider craftily made some advances towards the desired mate. I thought he well deserved the prize, but he too was given the brush-off. What I had not reckoned with is the fact that Spiders seldom quarrel and so the 'fighting' I watched was more probably males just showing off their prowess and muscle-power.

The female Spider is a most loyal lover. Those three males were being repulsed simply because they were outsiders. A female Spider can tell when her accepted admirer is 'on the line' because he has his own secret 'twitch' on the strand of web and his lady responds with her own signal, saying in effect 'it's OK dear to come up and see me'!

A naturalist friend has done some remarkable mathematical calculations with Spiders' webs. Believe it or not, in a web say 30cms. across the total length of line is over 30 metres. Each web line is made from six threads, and each thread consists of a thousand strands, so the entire web accounts for around 76 miles of silken strand. And all this stupendous work is completed in just over one hour, yet another example of the wonders of Nature (not surprising that Robert Bruce, King of Scotland, and many others since have held up the energetic little Spider as the essence of perseverance).

Woodland antics

BY SPECIAL REQUEST from one of my regular BBC Radio Lincolnshire listeners I visited some mixed woodland on the Boston side of Grantham to hear, and perhaps see, the Wood-Lark said to be singing there.

I had my doubts about all this since the common Tree-Pipit is often mistakenly called a Wood-Lark and, what is more, the bird I wanted to see is very local in distribution and from southern England it gets scarcer the further north you go. If what I had been told was true, I knew the Wood-Lark would most likely be around the outskirts of the dense woodland since it is, despite taking refuge in the trees, distinctly a ground bird in its habits. Anyway, sure enough, I heard in those woods the rich song of the Wood-Lark; it is even richer in tone than the Skylark but less varied. I was well rewarded for my journey, not only by hearing this bird but, by way of a bonus, by seeing that slatey-backed and white-chinned bird, the Nuthatch.

Making a sound something like *'whit-whit, whit-whit'*, the Nuthatch flew to a tree stump and proceeded to eat a Hazel nut – first rather cleverly jamming it tight in a crevice. The Nuthatch brought his curved bill down on the nut with his full force and when the nut at first failed to crack open, the bird just stopped and stared at it — head on one side and a perplexed expression on his face for all the world as though the bird was saying to himself 'you're just being awkward!'

Poised in this perplexity, the Nuthatch looked very beautiful, tints of delicate blue mixing in perfect tone with his white, chestnut-red and slate-grey feathers. But the Nuthatch is by no means only a pretty boy! Suddenly, with a shake of his sturdy body, the bird again attacked the obstinate and hard Hazel nut and this time he certainly 'cracked the job'. Chips of shell splintered around the tree stump and his meal was ready.

Field and Stream magazine's reviewer felt that D.H. Lawrence's account of an English gamekeeper's daily life, in *Lady Chatterley's Lover,* was 'full of considerable interest to outdoor-minded readers, as it contains many passages on pheasant raising, the apprehending of poachers, ways to control vermin and other chores and duties of the professional gamekeeper. Unfortunately, one is obliged to wade through many pages of extraneous material in order to discover and savour these sidelights on the management of a Midland estate'.

November

I am not a Foxhunting man, but as that season begins on November 1st and this book was compiled around the time of a General Election, I thought it quite appropriate to head this chapter with Bismarck's classic remark...
'People never lie so much as after a hunt, during a war and before an election'.

Late departures

EACH YEAR I seem to get a spate of telephone calls commenting on what I have said the previous month about the departure dates of Swallows, Swifts and Martins. As late in the year as November 3rd one listener said she had seen a Swift near Gainsborough despite the fact that Swifts are usually the first to leave for warmer climates, early in August as a rule. November is certainly very late, but even so a sighting this month is not quite a record as I know of at least one reference in bird manuals to Swifts being seen as late as December 13th.

Another listener, living in Nottingham, asked if it was true that Swifts are never off the wing. In other words, do they stay airborne day and night? Furthermore, he wanted to know whether it was true that the Swift sometimes flies as high as 7,000 metres. Contrary to popular belief, it is *not* true that Swifts are never off the wing; occasionally they can be seen resting on the ground and then succeeding in taking off again. It was that great ornithologist T.A. Coward who proved the point by placing captured Swifts on the ground and then watching the birds raise their long, pointed and powerful wings high above their heads and – with a single strong downwards stroke – lift themselves into the air without any preliminary take-off shuffling along the ground. Vertical take-off, no less, and one more reason to justify the Swift's claim to be our most acrobatic bird:

> *Like a rushing comet sable*
> *Swings the wide-winged screaming swift...*

How high up can a Swift go? I just do not know and I doubt whether anyone else does either, any more than we know for sure whether Swifts sleep on the wing or return to roost after dark. It seems more than likely that, like the Albatross sea bird (whose wings are vastly bigger but much the same shape as those of the Swift) that Swifts glide and sleep in steady air currents without having to flap their wings.

Except when the Swift ascends high into the sky for play – and play they most certainly do – the altitude of their flight is determined by the height at which insects are flying and this is why countrymen find Swifts and Swallows to be very reliable weather forecasters. When rain is coming the insects, and therefore the birds catching them, fly low over the ground; in dry settled conditions they fly high up. It is, nevertheless, true that some insects are out and about in the rain and Swifts often feed during a storm; so much so that folklore has it that the bird brings bad weather, hence calling it the Devil-bird.

A Thing of Beauty...

SOME PEOPLE refer to this month as 'grey November' – a melancholy, depressing month with cold, overcast skies. They, and the poets who sing doleful ditties about the approach of winter, go on moaning right through until April unlocks the flowers! But, when all is said and done, if you *look* for the grey in life then you will nearly always find it. The countryman's view is quite different; he knows we can enjoy any weather if only we get out of doors and are properly clad for it.

Anytime from early November onwards we can expect fresh-water ponds to freeze over, even if only briefly. Water plants may look as though they are dying, discoloured leaves floating on the surface or stuck in ice. But down below all is well. The estate lake I so frequently visit at Belvoir now presents a very different picture from July time when it was a glorious sight covered with waxy-looking Water Lilies, both yellow and white. The flowers and luscious leaves may have gone now, but anchored to the lake bottom waiting until it is time, year after year, to send up new leaves and new flowers. The fish in the lake – they, too, are busy just now adapting their haunts to the approach of winter, mainly by seeking deeper water and becoming less active to conserve energy for better days to come.

The poet John Keats might have been writing about this Belvoir lake with its summertime floating carpet of exotic colour – I wonder if you remember his lines in the romance *Endymion*, declaring that *'a thing of beauty is a joy for ever'* and continuing:

> Its loveliness increases; it will never
> Pass into nothingness; but still will keep
> A bower quiet for us, and a sleep
> Full of sweet dreams, and health and quiet breathing.

Walking away from the lakeside on my last visit I headed for one of our old village inns and there I was told that Hawfinches were around the canal locks. Another mile to walk, but well worth the effort; my friend was right and I was lucky enough to catch a glimpse of this particularly shy and and secretive bird the Hawfinch which, in some odd way I have never understood, seems to avoid man but not his dwellings. Earlier in the autumn Hawfinches will enter gardens and orchards and peck at well-coloured ripe fruit but I forgive them – as much as anything because they are such odd looking birds.

In case you do not happen to know what a Hawfinch looks like I can describe him as being rather top-heavy with a big head, huge bill and stumpy tail. And he has an ungentlemanly, penetrating whistle! But make no mistake about it, the Hawfinch is a strong bird and in his thick bill he can turn a fruit stone and split it in half. His dress? Well, that is in keeping with his slightly vulgar shape – a drab brown shading to greyish dirty white.

The Hawfinch may be a thieving Mr Quilp of birds but it was nice to see him among all those elegant Goldfinches, Bramblings and Greenfinches busy on the Teasel heads and fluffy seed of Sow Thistles along the old Viking Way beside the canal.

Hedge trimmings

LIKE farmers at this time of year, I trim all the thorn hedges around the cottage. I say 'thorn' but if truth be told these hedges contain plenty of Ash saplings, stunted Elderberry and Ivy – in particular, the Ivy is thick where long ago there used to be gateways into what is now a garden but was then pig-sties. In November this Ivy seems to support about half the insect kingdom and the reason is obvious; the succession of new creamy-coloured flowerheads on Ivy offer plenty of nectar for insects with short tongues. The Ivy also seem to attract lots of flies and, when the day is sunny, a few late Wasps show great interest in the big 'blue-bottles' and other flies.

The first indication that a Wasp has found a victim is a frantic buzzing, like a fly caught in a Spider's web. As it pounces, the Wasp curls its belly round the fly, trying to sting it; then, joined together, Wasp and 'blue-bottle' topple into the hedge bottom. Next a very odd thing happens: after killing the fly the victor Wasp is often joined by another and together the Wasps pull the fly apart for a tasty meal.

Not all my hedges are well-trimmed, any more than are all the farm hedges, and this is not the bad thing you may think. For conservation reasons, I leave some hedges almost untouched, particularly where Teasel and other large seed heads attract the Goldfinch, or Thistlefinch as the descriptive country name has it. To see that glossy red throat, and black and yellow wings, of a Goldfinch flitting about brings joy to my heart. Because of its light and buoyant way of flying, the sociable little Goldfinch is sometimes called the 'fairy bird', and aptly enough the proper collective name for a number of these birds is 'a charm of Goldfinch'.

To this, and my full reference list of Terms for Groups of Wildlife (see page 129), one or two delightful additions can be made thanks to Mr S. Dernley, of Mansfield, who has for years been recording examples of collective nouns which seem to be disappearing from common use. A new one to me is 'an explosion of Partridge' – very descriptive this, as anyone who has ever started up a covey in the field will agree. Nothing to do with wildlife, but I also very much like another new one – 'a bottom of cyclists'. Splendid!

Although the songsters among our wild birds are largely silent by this time of year (except, of course, for the Robin Redbreast, bless him) there is still a great deal of noise and chattering from the Starlings in the top of the very high old Pear tree in the cottage orchard, as well as from Rooks and Lapwings in the long meadow. There is, in fact, a lot of bird activity around just now, particularly in the occasional field still unploughed after corn harvest. I see these fields covered with flocks of Sparrows, Linnets and Chaffinches, although I get the impression that the colourful little Chaffinches are nowhere as common as they used to be.

In the newly-ploughed fields Starlings outnumber every other species, as indeed they do in the tops of the Elm trees behind the farm windmill. I look out across what I call our 'Rowland Hilder view' in our hamlet of so few homesteads and see the trees black with what must amount to hundreds of chattering Starlings. He may not be in the Goldfinch class, but the Starling – apart from his nuisance value in eating grain I put out for the poultry and driving less aggressive birds from the garden bird table – is not unattractive with its shiny speckled plumage. I regard Starlings as bossy birds, well described by a friend's remark that 'they strut about looking like schoolmasters, their pointed wings resembling academic gowns!'

Starlings are, of course, resident birds of the U.K. and when their numbers become excessive it is usually due to a big influx of winter visitors from the Continent. Occasionally I have seen Starlings flying in military-style formation, hundreds strong, and the birds spaced in oblong, square or diamond-shaped groups and flying at even speeds as though, in army parlance, dressing by the right. Other observers have said that this usually happens when a Sparrowhawk flies through the Starlings' territory, the Starlings grouping to one side of the hawk's flight path to see it off.

This month Starlings are joined by Fieldfares and Redwings, also from Northern Europe and here to enjoy the bounteous supplies of Hawthorn and other berries in the hedgerows. Other native birds whose numbers fluctuate at this time of year are Rooks and Lapwings, usually moving from one part of the country to another in search of food. Among the Rooks we have our own 'regulars' from a small rookery a mile down the lane and they arrive at almost the same time every morning to eat acorns beneath a group of Oak trees and they depart at an equally set time in the afternoons.

More often than not Rooks fly to feeding grounds in an east to west direction rather than north to south and this was a phenomenon commented on by the naturalist Richard Jefferies (to whose works I have referred before in this book). Jefferies suggested that Rooks have their own laws handed down from generation to generation. They have their *traditional* feeding grounds, often ignoring other and more profitable fields nearby. By the same token it seems that tradition might determine their flight direction since, long ago, this was found to be the best route to rich feeding grounds: today's birds follow the same route although the forest has long since gone from the fields to which these cottage Rooks of ours come each day. I am glad to say however, there are enough trees left for the birds still to get a meal of acorns, beechmast and chestnuts.

There are few places this month where you can better see Nature evolving before your eyes than along the Lincolnshire coastal sand-dunes. With the stormy weather November often brings, it is a particularly good time to observe the changes in shape and size of sand-dunes and to think on the intimate part played in the process of plants. Any plant, such as Marram and Couch Grass, which can gain a hold in the shifting world of sand must have stupendous survival technique. And, incidentally, when you are next walking the dunes do have a look around the sand beyond the reach of the tide; even as late in the year as this I have found such winter annuals as Forget-me-Not, Chickweed and Whitlow Grass.

City centres are also rich in wildlife evolution and changes of habitat. From time to time I find myself at the Barbican Arts Centre, in the City of London, and much to my delight this formerly war-devastated part of London has become a haven of wildlife. I have seen on the lake at the Barbican not only the expected Mallard and Tufted Duck, but even a Heron resting on top of Gilbert House. And around the ornamental shrubs there are Wrens, Goldfinches and Wagtails – how happy they help to make my day!

The pity is that so few city folk appear to have eyes to see such delights or ears to hear them – which reminds me of a townsman I met whilst travelling to BBC Lincolnshire by train and who, without any preliminary remarks, suddenly asked me if I was aware of the noise aspect of the conflict between town and country? 'Not particularly, why?' says I. 'Damn it man' says the stranger, 'I'm thinking of retreating back to the city because of it.' I tried to show not the slightest interest in *where* he chose to live, but he battled on, explaining that he was merely one of the 'droves of people misled enough to move into the country to escape the sounds and smells of the town.' But what did they find? In the city gentleman's own words -

> Cows keep mooing. Tractors and machines clatter from six in the mornings. Chain-saws rip. Grain driers chunter. Weaned lambs baa all night long. And right now the air is saturated with the stink of farmyard muck being spread on the fields. What next, man? What next?

I was never more thankful to see St Mark's station at Lincoln, and enjoy my lone walk up Steep Hill!

Not all Beatrix Potter

GREY SQUIRRELS running up and down the branches of woodland trees are a plentiful sight this month. There are also a fair number of dead, squashed ones on the road but I shed no tears over these deaths because I do not believe good can be said about this alien animal (apart, I suppose, from children who can regard him as a pretty little creature with a lovely bushy tail, and a few fishermen clever enough to tie flies from the tail hairs!)

The truth is that the no doubt well-meaning folk who let loose imported Grey Squirrels into their parks in the 1890s have much to answer for. The Grey Squirrel has spread rapidly everywhere and has replaced our own much more attractive Red Squirrel. The Grey Squirrel is a pest to foresters and fruit growers; it also eats the eggs and young of small birds, especially the beneficial insect-eating species.

In talking with naturalists, foresters and gamekeepers about what is often called the 'tree rat' some conflicting ideas come out. For one thing, the Grey Squirrel is not a rat – although all Squirrels belong to the rodents as do Rabbits and Hares – and nobody calls them rats! The second common fallacy is that the Grey Squirrel, which first came from America, drove out the Red Squirrel from our woods. The main reason for the decline of the Red Squirrel was disease, aided by the cutting down of forests, and the Red Squirrel became almost extinct in Britain long before the arrival of the grey type.

Unlike the Red Squirrel, which prefers Pine and Fir trees, the grey is at home anywhere and it is seen on the ground much more. It often scurries for miles over open ground and I have even seen one eating the food off a bird table near the centre of Nottingham.

Years ago I had a small fruit and poultry farm in Essex and these pesty Grey Squirrels were so eager to get at the sap of some new Worcester Pearmain apples I had planted that they gnawed a band of bark right round the trunks. This, of course, stopped the sap rising to the upper branches and all the trees died within a year. Some people say they could not shoot 'a pretty little Grey Squirrel'. After that orchard episode I certainly can.

Earlier this year, after the very mild 1982-83 winter, the Forestry Commission warned farmers and landowners that the numbers of Grey Squirrels was expected to increase substantially. Unfortunately, our native broadleaved trees between ten and forty years old are particularly at risk from these destructive animals gnawing away at the bark.

Winter visitors

FOOD for the birds now becomes scarce and once the ground is frozen birds have quite literally to 'scratch for a living'. In cold weather birds need food not only to survive, but to keep warm. It was largely to avoid starvation that the Swallows and Swifts left us for the southern hemisphere, where the supply of insects will not be frozen up, and in their place we shall enjoy not only our residents but also the company of birds from Arctic regions coming here for our more temperate climate.

Winter visitors fall into two groups, water birds and land birds. The water birds, various Ducks and Geese among them, find their food on unfrozen estuaries around our coasts, on lakes and in the water meadows; the land birds, including the familiar Redwing and the Fieldfare, will be seen in flocks feeding on seeds and berries. If you are walking around coastal estuaries, or sometime even around inland lakes, you may see the orange-billed Bean Goose and the Pink-Footed Goose as well as the more usual Brent Goose, easily recognisable from his habit of grovelling in the wet mud with his whole neck and head searching for bits of plant delicacies.

An attractive land species to watch for is the Brambling, a striking looking member of the Finch family and very friendly with Chaffinches. Bramblings often move around in flocks, particularly where there is any beech-mast, their favourite food. This bird comes to us from the pine forests of Northern Europe and can be recognised from its lovely glossy blue-black head and neck and two white stripes on buff-coloured wings.

When you educate a man, you educate an individual; but when you educate a woman you educate a family.

Gandhi

December

Snow is beautiful

DECEMBER, when the sun is in the ninth zodiac sign of the year – Sagittarius the Archer. Not the month when we get either the coldest weather of the winter or the most snow, but to many the thought of a white Christmas is attractive and somehow regarded as being seasonal, typical of the traditional scene on Christmas cards. In fact, Christmas weather is on average over the years much more likely to be mild and 'green', even in those years when it has snowed earlier in the month – as early as the 13th in the particular December in which I was born; the snow was over a foot deep as I arrived on the scene at five o'clock that Saturday morning, and they say it went on snowing most of the day!

Snow – beautiful or a nuisance? I suppose your view depends partly on where you live, town or country, and the kind of work you do. I personally share the view of the great naturalists that there is nothing in the entire range of inorganic Nature more lovely than a fall of snow in the fields and woods. Men who thought like this include Gilbert White, the clergyman of Selborne fame who wrote so joyously but scientifically about Nature, and William Henry Hudson who came from America and wrote some of the most enduring classics of the English countryside. Certainly I do not understand people who *pither* indoors moaning all the time there is snow about and only waiting for a thaw (incidentally, do you know that word *pither*? I cannot find it in any of my dictionaries but I learned it from an old Lincolnshire Wolds shepherd and I think it exactly conveys the picture of an unoccupied, fidgeting person).

It might help you to enjoy a fall of snow if you find out about the beauty of snow-flakes and the lovely stellar ice-flowers which, grouped together, form those flakes. These perfect transparent stars are of infinite variety and from a pin-head upwards in size. Just catch a few snow-flakes on your sleeve and look at them through a strong magnifying glass: you will see that they are, in fact, clusters of crystals of ice and all hexagonal – a shape which occurs in petals of flowers and in the cells of Bees and Wasps. The reason may well be, but here I am only guessing, that of all the polygons (in other words, shapes with more than four sides) inscribed in a circle the hexagon is the only one whose sides are equal to the radius of the circle and whose *angles give the most space with the minimum of matter!*)

In snow crystals each star usually has six rays coming out from the centre and it is the joining up of these rays that results in the hexagon shape – and yet, believe it or not, no two of the millions of tiny ice-crystals are precisely the same! The crystals 'grow' as they float through the air and hundreds of them form as a snow-flake. This is why I say that snow is beautiful, quite apart from various practical benefits it gives – including the fact that as snow flakes fall they gather up from the air a good deal of soluble and suspended impurities, leaving the atmosphere purer and sweeter: this accounts for the feeling of well-being one gets from exercise in the snow. The farmer and gardener get a bonus too; the falling snow-flakes pick up a certain amount of nitrogen from the air and this is carried into the soil when a thaw comes.

When I am out enjoying myself in the snow I remember some lines of verse written a long time ago by a poet (name unknown) who was then sweltering under a blistering sun on an island in the Indian Ocean:

> *God! for the sound of an English breeze –*
> *with its welcome winter blow!*
> *God! for the sight of an English silver birch –*
> *its branches covered with snow!*
> *For an English field in winter white,*
> *For an English sky with the ray of light*
> *of a sunset afterglow.*

So why not think on that and if there is snow about do not 'pither' indoors any longer!

How to feed birds

THE BRIGHTEST splash of colour in early December days is without doubt the gorgeous electric-blue of Kingfishers around the lakes or darting over the little River Devon as it flows under the bridge just below the cottage.

Another bird delight is the *'twink, twink'* of Chaffinches, this call repeated again and again as they feed on beech-mast lying beneath the Autumn fallen leaves. It is an interesting fact, but not one often commented upon by naturalists, that the plumage of birds after they have been feeding on beech-mast for a time takes on a satin gloss. I presume this is due to the amount of oil in the nuts.

Time now to feed the birds in the garden and, like everything else, there is a right and a wrong way to do so. To start with, not everyone who has a garden necessarily *likes* gardening (something which totally passes my comprehension but as the saying goes 'it takes all sorts') so here is a tip to give reluctant gardeners some comfort; you can help feed birds by not completely tidying up the garden in early winter and the reason is, of course, that many of the seeds, fruits and insects left on all those weeds and other rubbish are just what the birds need as the weather gets colder.

Experts say that the best winter bird foods are bones (because of the marrow in them); fat and suet; pieces of bacon rind; cheese (I find this a favourite with Wrens and Robins); oats and oatmeal; bird seed as used for canaries; apples; baked potatoes and, if you can spare it, a bit of your dog or cat food. And now what *not* to feed to the birds: white bread, *unless soaked in water,* and chopped up coconut can swell in the bird's crop and choke them. Salted peanuts are also dangerous but the *unsalted* kind are good.

A bird table is the simplest way to feed birds, and ideally it should have a roof to keep the food dry. There are other feeding devices, such as wire baskets for nuts, and it is worth while getting the catalogue of garden bird equipment issued by the Royal Society for the Protection of Birds, The Lodge, Sandy, Bedfordshire.

In very bad weather put out some food (and do not forget some water) for the birds both first thing in the morning and again in the afternoon. Should you scatter the food on the ground then do it in the open because around shrubs and trees there is always the risk of prowling cats. At the cottage we hang up our own speciality for the birds called tit-cake: simply render down 2 lbs of suet and into the hot fat pour 1 lb. of unsalted peanuts. Let the mixture set hard in a dish or metal pan and there is the tit-cake! Hang the cake outside where it can be easily seen from a window and the birds will flock to it.

Garden or no garden, the food which you can put out for birds can be vital to their survival in winter. I stress *winter* because, out of mistaken kindness, some townsfolk put out bird food all the year round. This is not a good thing to do. From nesting time in April to, say, September, young birds can actually be harmed by bread crumbs and other house scraps. In Spring and early summer young birds will do much better on natural food than anything you can provide.

Romany friends

THERE ARE few wild animals to be seen at this time of year when many are either hibernating or seeking deeper cover from Man and weather now that the woods are leafless and open ploughed fields offer no shelter.

The Badger and the Hedgehog are often thought of as hibernating in winter but this is only partly true and I have seen both animals out and about in December. Badgers may appear sluggish in movement and stay in their sets for up to three days at a time, but they are still awake and by next month a pair will be preparing a set for a new litter of cubs.

Hedgehogs stay asleep only from the end of October to about March if the winter is severe; otherwise out they occasionally come in search of food – particularly if they have had their sleep disturbed in some way and feel hungry. As a young man beginning my professional career in Kent, I saw gipsies dig up sleeping Hedgehogs to eat, first slicing off the spines and removing the stomachs as deftly as a fishmonger fillets a fish! I even accepted an invitation (very rarely given to a *gorgio*, or non-gypsy) to try a bit of *hotchiwitchi* (Hedgepig in our language).

I should explain that ever since I was 'kneehigh to a Grasshopper', as the country phrase goes, sitting for hours watching narrowboats on the

Trent and Mersey Canal gliding softly by at the foot of my grandparents' garden lawn in Burton-on-Trent, I have been fascinated by the characters and life-styles of both the narrowboat families living on the water and the Romany families living in wagons on the road. I do not have a proper knowledge of the ancient Romani language but, from my long collected library of books about these people, I have learned a few Romani words and they have come in very useful as you will gather from what I am about to tell you. For instance, I know that *Bori-diklo* means a lady's head-scarf and this word I used when admiring a nice example worn by a young and very striking raven-haired *chai* (woman) whom I once came across nodding off to sleep beside an iron pot in which the traditional *hotchiwitchi* were being boiled.

I could hardly have been more successful if I had serenaded her with that charming old ballad *Slumber on my little gipsy sweetheart* since my bit of Romani led to me being invited to share their meal and, on a return visit a few days later, also trying Hedgehog roasted in clay. By this time, thoroughly enjoying myself, I began to get Matthew Arnold-like illusions of perhaps becoming a scholar-gipsy! The memory came back to me of my son, whilst showing promise at a grammar school of old foundation, expressing to a careers master the wish of becoming what he called 'an educated tramp' and I began to wonder if these dissenting nomadic traits had been bred in the bone (perhaps through some earlier individual's misguided choice of partner?) I decided to wish my Romany friends *Kushit-Bok* (Good Luck!) and went away, reciting happily to myself all I could remember of Matthew Arnold's lovely but long poem:

> And near me on the grass lies Glanvil's book -
> Come, let me read the oft-read tale again!
> The story of that Oxford scholar poor,
> Of shining parts and quick inventive brain,
> Who, tired of knocking at preferment's door,
> One summer-morn forsook
> His friends, and went with that wild brotherhood,
> And came, as most men deem'd, to little good,
> But came to Oxford and his friends no more.

Now back from literary (and other) flights of fancy to the study of zoology and, in particular, animal hibernation. Contrary to general belief, very few mammals truly hibernate, but the tiny Dormouse is one who does. And how very soundly he sleeps; I once tried wakening a hibernating Dormouse but no amount of prodding, or even rolling him about on a table, had the slightest effect. My Dormouse slept on, the soundest of all animal sleepers.

At the start of winter in November, and choosing a nesting site in the bole of a tree, or even in an old bird's nest if it is near the ground, the

Dormouse rolls up and somehow manages to cover himself with a perfect ball of moss and grass, with apparently no entrance or way out. They surround themselves with a good store of nuts – usually Hazel. (Incidentally, although normally thought of as a shrub, in Scotland Hazels are found growing as large trees.)

Very pretty little chap is the Dormouse, with his reddish-brown coat. He is like a miniature Squirrel in both colour and agility, with a long bushy tail and a similar way of nibbling his food. This tiny creature has no fear. Before hibernation, I have watched a Dormouse running along a tree branch in search of nuts, wild cherries and other winter fruits. I stood still in full view of the Dormouse who just continued about his business quite regardless of me.

Silent waters

AS FAR AS flowers are concerned this month, on mild days you may well find the normally February-flowering Coltsfoot and Celandines, apart from Daisies, Chickweed and Groundsel which can be found flowering in most months of the year. Hazel catkins are worth noticing and the catkins showing now are the male ones, about an inch long and delicate green in colour. Until the Spring, these male Hazel catkins will remain dormant, then, in early March, they swell and ripen into the fluffy Pussy Willow, or 'lambs tails' as children used to call them.

Before getting too busy with Christmas preparations I have long made it my custom to have a late walk around the lakes and year after year, as though discovering it for the first time, I am most of all struck by the utter silence. Can any place, I wonder, be as remote and as still as a lake on a quiet winter's day?

Silent it may be, but that does not mean to say there is nothing to see. On the contrary, it is one of winter's great country pleasures to watch water birds arriving and feeding on inland lakes and ponds. I can always reckon on seeing quite a few different species, including Mallard, Teal, Widgeon, Canada Geese and Pochard; all these apart, of course, from such plentiful regulars as Moorhen, Coot and Heron. Note how Ducks swim powerfully straight through surface water weed however thick it is, but the Moorhen and Coot trip daintily across the top of floating leaves.

I suppose the most interesting ducks are those that dive to feed rather than, say, the Mallard which gets its food on or near the surface of the water. Of the diving birds the Pochard is fairly easy to find at this time of the winter. The male Pochard's plumage is very distinctive, his red head at once catching the eye, a startling contrast to the delicate lavender grey of the rest of his upper feathers. The Pochard, sometimes called by countrymen the Red-headed Poker, is a winter visitor, although a few of these birds from the far frozen North stay and breed here in the Spring, notably in parts of Yorkshire.

If you want to watch Pochard feeding, then try visiting a lake just as it gets dark. You will probably see them enjoying themselves with other species on the surface of the water; then, quite suddenly, the Pochard disappear without a sound; they have dived to the bottom of the water to feed off water-weed or to search for water insects and small shellfish. Then, up they bob for a few seconds only to vanish again like magic as before. I have also watched these birds make a most graceful curved spring into the air before swooping down into the lake out of sight.

Should the pond you intend to visit be very sheltered, perhaps in a wood, then you will most likely find the Teal, the smallest of our wild ducks. A sheltered pond is his favourite haunt, so look our for a bird with a chestnut coloured head across which a curved green patch runs from the bird's eye to the back of his neck. The rest of the Teal's feathers are grey with brown mottlings and a long white streak on his wings. A shooting man knows it takes a good eye to hit a Teal, so fast do they fly, twisting and turning about. A flock of these nice little birds is called a 'spring of Teal' and a fascinating sight it is.

Christmas lore

BY THE third week in December, most people are busy putting up the Christmas decorations and it is time to think about those plants from our countryside which are so much a traditional part of our lives from childhood onwards.

What we are pleased to call a Christmas tree is, to give its proper name, a Norway Spruce and the practice of decorating it with gifts and lights was introduced from Germany in 1844 by Prince Albert, Queen Victoria's consort. The true Christmas tree is our own familiar Holly, one of the very few native British evergreens, the name of which is a corruption of the word Holy. In folklore, both the Holly and the Ivy were supposed to be plants of power. It was long thought that Holly in the home warded off demons, witches and house-goblins, and in the county of Hampshire they went one better still, believing that whooping cough could be cured if children drank milk from a cup made from Holly wood. In parts of the Middle East it was the custom to sprinkle an infusion of Holly leaves to endow young children with great wisdom.

Working the Holly into early Christian beliefs was not difficult: Holly is thorny and its berries are scarlet, so it came to symbolise Christ's crown of thorns and his blood. And, religion apart, there are some odd customs involving Holly, like the one on Boxing Day at Tenby in South Wales where, years ago, men and youths went Holly-beating and the idea was to run through the streets hitting girls on their hands and arms. No more odd I suppose than some of the pagan rites attached to Mistletoe, many of them stemming from the eighteenth and nineteenth centuries' mania for Druid customs.

In the East Midlands there were few people more involved with the Druid scene than a Mr William Stukeley of Grantham. In his garden he contrived a Druid temple in an old orchard, the temple being complete with imitation Stonehenge circles and lots of Mistletoe, something Mr Stukeley and other Druids maintained was a 'heavenly plant'. The Druids believed this because Mistletoe does not grow *on* the earth but flourishes *up* in the branches of a host tree; this fact was translated as being symbolic of Man's dependence upon God. Other strange beliefs about Mistletoe ranged from its legendary powers to increase women's sexual desires, to curing barrenness in cattle and being a useful antidote to many poisons. And time was when it was thought that a sprig of Mistletoe worn under your hat gave protection against witchcraft.

But enough of Grantham's Mr Stukeley. Just as much nonsense occurs in all manner of Christmas folk-tales and popular verse of days now gone. For instance:

> *He who eats twelve mince-pies*
> *In twelve different houses during*
> *The Twelve Days of Christmas*
> *Will have twelve Happy Months*
> *In the coming year.*

December is said to be the darkest month of all. December the 21st is the shortest day of the year in terms of daylight hours but after that, however imperceptible at first, the hours of daylight lengthen and it takes only an hour or so of pale, winter sunshine to cheer us up.

At the end of the old year and the beginning of the new is the time a countryman keeps his eyes open on the chance of being lucky enough to glimpse one or more of a rare trio of bird visitors – the Crossbill, the Nutcracker and the Waxwing. These three very handsome birds are not normal migrants, but in severe weather conditions in Scandinavia and Russia they do occasionally fly into Britain. We saw Crossbills in Larch trees in the mid-December snow of 1981, when conditions lasting until after Christmas were the coldest for over 30 years.

A flea and a fly in the flue
Were imprisoned, so what could they do?
Said the flea, 'Let us fly!'
Said the fly, 'Let us flee!'
So they flew through a flaw in the flue.

January

Long knowledge

BY THE CALENDAR, the first day of this month starts the New Year but, as I said earlier in this book, Nature's new year started in October. Then began the period of rest which goes on through this month and next before Spring comes again in March – the month when everything is about to happen, hence starting *Our Country Year* that particular month. Now it is January and even if it is the coldest of the twelve months I like to recall those lines by the eighteenth century poet William Cowper so justly renowned for his sensitive descriptions of Nature:

> *Scenes must be beautiful which, daily roamed*
> *Please daily, and whose novelty survives*
> *Long knowledge and the scrutiny of years.*

It may seem that in January there are but few pleasing scenes in the sleeping countryside, but this is true only up to a point: to the experienced eye (or what Cowper called 'long knowledge') there are happy signs of the early awakening of life, particularly in such trees as

Lime, Sycamore, Elder and Lilac. We have some Honeysuckle growing up into a Silver Birch tree and even as early as January the Honeysuckle begins to open its leaf buds. The Holly, too, shows little cream-coloured flower buds and there are still a few red berries on the Hawthorn, but few is the operative word since Fieldfares and the Redwings have had their Christmas and New Year feasts.

This month of January is the best time to observe the fascinating Tree Creeper. He is so well camouflaged that at other times of the year the Tree Creeper is lost from sight among the boughs and leaves of trees where he is busy probing for insects. Now it is easy to see this bird begin searching for food at the base of a tree and then working his way up the trunk in a series of rapid spiral movements, relying for support on his stiff tail and wide-gripping feet. Out on a country walk should you hear a call something like *'see, see, see, sissy-pee'* look up the bark of the nearest big tree and you may find a Tree Creeper at work.

Staying with the wild birds, here are a few further notes from my diary about the Crossbills, Nutcrackers and Waxwings I mentioned in December. Despite the 'doubting Thomas' who might disbelieve claims to have seen these birds here, they have in fact been coming to Britain in severe continental winters for hundreds of years and the oldest recording dates from the thirteenth century. We know that occasional invasions of these birds are the result of conditions hundreds of miles to the north and east in the great coniferous forests of Russia and northern Scandinavia. There, although the forests are composed of vast numbers of trees they are of relatively few types. In the case of the Crossbill its life is intimately connected with the Spruce tree – if there has been a poor harvest of Spruce seeds these birds gather and fly off to other areas.

The place to look for a Nutcracker is also in woodland, but not confined to coniferous trees. The Nutcracker is fond of Hazel nuts and it is easy enough to find a coppice with plenty of these small trees. Watch for a chocolate-brown bird, not unlike a Jay with their slow, undulating flight, and prominent white spots on its feathers. Not many Hazel nuts near our cottage, but the Nutcracker does occasionally turn up looking for acorns from the Oaks.

In contrast to Crossbills and Nutcrackers, the Waxwing – also a resident of northern Russia – is a berry-eater. This most handsome bird gets its name from the waxy red tips to its secondary feathers and it loves the berries on Guelder Rose in the hedgerows or on those solid lumps of land called Alder carrs in our eastern fen and marshes. Not common by any means, and yet at intervals it has come here in quite big numbers. Something I have never understood is why the Waxwing used to be called the Bohemian Chatterer – in fact, it is a totally silent bird!

Crossbill on Larch

A two-faced month

THE MONTH of January was named after Janus, the two-faced Italian deity who looked both ways. He was usually represented with two heads looking in opposite directions; there is even something called a Januscloth, a fabric with different colours on opposite sides. It would seem, then, that it was no mere whim that led to Janus being the chosen symbol of January, since this is traditionally the time when man looks back as well as forwards and 'balances his books'. This month of Janus is indeed two-faced in its weather: it can, and does, bring snow and ice but it also brings some sunny skies and comparatively warm evenings, enough to bring out the winter midges.

On its mild, sunny days, when January seems to be imitating Spring, Blackbirds can be heard piping up to each other with news of worms rising to the surface of the soil; or a Thrush tunes up his vocal chords for the Song of Spring to come. But perhaps even more reassuring than bird song and the expanding buds on trees like the Ash, Alder and Aspen, is the sight of a few Daisies in the grass; the modest tiny flower that the poet said 'helps to paint the meadows with delight'.

During one of these short January sunny spells I visited the ruins of a woodman's cottage just inside Leicestershire at a spot where, later in the year, I shall find sumptious King Cups blazing yellow in the marsh below. I was delighted by an old bush of Jasmine in flower over what was left of the woodman's outdoor loo, more or less the only remaining evidence of what once was a home – albeit a home with a tragic history of murder. Around the sheltered base of the Jasmine a few Snowdrops were opening up, so creating for me a lovely picture in yellow, white and two shades of green.

Fair Maids

THE SNOWDROP – first recorded as wild in the 1770s in Worcestershire and certainly growing like such in a few secret places I know in Northamptonshire and Staffordshire – starts to flower in January, despite countrymen calling them the Fair Maids of February. This winter flower refuses to be molly-coddled and it thrives in snow and frost however frail it may look, with its hanging head concealing such exquisite shades of green and gold. The secret of this hardiness lies in the fact that the hanging bell of this flower holds a little pocket of air that is always a degree or two warmer than the air *outside* of the petals, so protecting the pollen from frost and wet.

Other fascinating phenomena of frost survival remain unexplained by botanists. For instance, the weird ability of the Witch Hazel (or *Hamamelis*) to flower however hard the weather, yet on the similar looking ordinary Hazel frost shrivels the catkins to cinders. Or take the lusty Stinging Nettle – it simply curls up and dies rather than be frost-bitten, yet the purple-flowered Dead Nettle (called 'dead' because it does not sting) goes on blooming quite happily.

On a January day I was closely watched by a man who stopped his cycle as I was walking into one of the meadows around our cottage. Even after going about my lawful business the stranger was still there on my return and point-blank asked me what I had been doing looking down into the grass so painstakingly. If it had been April, and I had been looking for a delicacy like Lapwing eggs, this stranger could not have been more aggressive in approach. I felt like telling him to mind his own business but I softened when he added 'after all, its only a field and I can't see anything in it except grass'. I felt sorry for him. Any countryman knows that a meadow is an exciting jungle of living creatures; the furry little Mole, for which I had been looking, is but one.

I made friends with the stranger and explained to him how, despite the very cold weather, the Moles had been busy throwing up heaps of finely sifted soil in their search for worms, slugs and insects. Moles are only about six inches long, weighing no more than three or four ounces, and yet with their powerful forelimbs they can excavate nearly five kilograms in twenty minutes. Worked out on a weight for weight basis, that is twelve times more material than a hefty coal miner can move with a pick and shovel! I explained to the stranger that the reason he saw me bending over so frequently in the meadow was because I was putting to the test this proverbial strength of the mole and to do so I had placed two house bricks on top of a jam-jar. What seemed impossible was done: the three-ounce Mole found no difficulty in toppling over the seven kilogram weight of bricks.

The best time to see Moles is either early in the morning, or on a damp evening. They live almost entirely underground in a system of tunnels rather like an underground railway. To make these tunnels the Moles thrust the soil ahead and, from time to time, push up the excavated soil – hence the familiar molehills we see in the fields (and on the lawn!). Regarding Moles, two very nice and little-known words spring to mind, both useful for Scrabble players or even for Frank Muir and his Call My Bluff television game! These words, still used in a few places in northern England, are 'tumps' for molehills and 'Mouldiwerp' for a Mole itself, this being derived from the Old English *molde* (meaning earth) and *werpen*, meaning to throw.

Moles have been unusually plentiful and busy this year. A Radio Lincolnshire listener living at Washingborough near Lincoln telephoned to say that she and her husband counted 140 tumps in an area of only about ten square metres. Oddly enough, and no doubt to the immense relief of bowls players, only a Beech hedge separated the molehill field from a bowling green but not a single heap of soil disturbed the pristine condition of the turf!

Mole-catching was once an easy and profitable business, the skins being used for making fur-coats, gloves and moleskin trousers and waistcoats. I am glad to say that such garments are no longer in fashion and the lovely little Mole is that much safer – even if they can be a nuisance on pasture land where the mounds of soil are apt to damage the blades of farmers' cutting machines.

Counting Magpies

I MYSELF do not have any particular 'thing' about Magpies, those black-and-white, long-tailed comics of the bird world – but it seems lots of other people do. Every so often letters appear in the correspondence columns of newspapers complaining of an increase in 'thieving Magpies'. Suggestions that Magpies are vermin and should be shot bring angry replies from other readers. All I know is that the Magpie is one of the most interesting birds in the Crow family, and shrouded in superstition.

Most of us heard as children the saying about Magpies:

> *One for sorrow,*
> *Two for joy,*
> *Three for a girl,*
> *Four for a boy.*

That is as far as I can go with the rhyme but I believe it went on up to at least seven or eight. After one of my broadcasts a listner 'phoned me with a very odd bit of advice; he said that if I was troubled with too many Magpies then I could alleviate the curse by saying 'Good-day your Lordship and how is her Ladyship?' That, said my listener, immediately lightens the sorrow!

some birds also seem to get ahead of schedule; at every mild opportunity they start singing their love ditties. In the middle of this month I often hear Blackbirds and Thrushes in full voice as though, happily shaking winter lassitude out of their feathers, they are determined to shut out the harsh *'chur-chur-chur'* flurry of notes from a Mistle-Thrush somewhere in the copse down by the river. As children we called this bird the Holm-Screech because he ate all the berries from the Holly, or Holm, at the gate entrance. And that reminds me of another bizarre event in family history as recorded in the historic diary I mentioned earlier. It seems that at Heanor, in Derbyshire, a doctor friend of my great-great-grandparents was thrown from his pony and trap, suffering a severe leg injury and subsequent amputation. The old gentleman insisted on his leg being ceremoniously buried under one of the Holly trees at the gates of our then family home!

The Mistle-Thrush, as I mentioned before, gets its name from the bird's particular fondness for the berries of Mistletoe, and at this time of year these birds settle down for the night in noisy flocks rather than their normal habit of roosting in pairs.

January – on average the coldest month of the year and time (if, like me, you are lucky enough to have an old-fashioned open fire as the focal point in your sitting room) to enjoy being warmed a second time by logs: the first warm up comes, of course, at the time you gather and saw up the logs on a crisp, frosty morning. So here, to end the month's notes, is a poetic distillation of country wisdom about burning different kinds of wood:

>Oak logs will warm you well
>   If they're old and dry.
>Larch logs of pinewood smell
>   But the sparks will fly.
>Beech logs for Christmas time,
>   Yew logs heat well.
>Scotch logs it is a crime
>   For anyone to sell.
>Birch logs burn too fast,
>   Chestnut scarce at all.
>Hawthorn logs are good to last
>   If you cut them in the fall.
>Holly logs will burn like wax,
>   You should burn them green.
>Elm logs like smouldering flax,
>   No flame to be seen.
>Pear logs and apple logs,
>   They will scent your room.
>Cherry logs across the dogs
>   Smell like flowers in bloom.
>But ash logs, all smooth and gray,
>   Burn them green or old:
>Buy up all that come your way,
>   They're worth their weight in gold.

February

The bush telegraph

ONE of the advantages of having so many friends in different counties spread over the East Midlands region all sharing an interest in, and good knowledge of, life in the countryside is that we can operate a kind of bush telegraph system. News quickly gets through to me of any rare bird sightings, unusual wild flowers or even the exact whereabouts of good shoals of fish – and off I go to see for myself.

The most recent occasion on which this bush telegraph worked well (one of its central 'exchanges' is, as you might expect, the village inn) it informed me of parties of Fire-Crested Wrens in a spinney on the Nottinghamshire borders. This bird, with its rich orange-yellow crest, is a rather scarce winter visitor and, to me, it was certainly worth a few miles to go and see them. I was a little doubtful as to whether my friend had perhaps confused these lovely little birds with *Golden-Crested Wrens*, easy enough to do. But he was right; there, darting erratically in pairs to and fro on Gorse bushes, were the Fire-Crests. There is a sure way of telling these birds apart. The Gold-Crest is the smallest of all British and even European birds, measuring only three inches (or should I say 76.2 millimetres) from beak to tail. The adult male has a golden frontal band which joins up with a white streak over the eye and this separates a parallel black line enclosing the orange crest. The difference comes in the amount of orange feathering – the Fire-Crest has much more than the Gold-Crest. A most delightful spectacle, whichever of these Wrens you manage to see.

The ordinary Wren is a garden favourite and even he is so small he can live in and around a garden for years without being seen very often. Instead of advertising his presence in the blatant manner of the Robin, a Wren survives by retreating from view if he thinks you are looking at him and promptly flies off into his favourite sulking place – stumps of old Ivy in the hedge is our own Wren's favourite. Disturb a Wren and he promptly calls out in a high-pitched *'tie-tie-tie'* to ward off intruders. In a long cold spell a number of Wrens will sometimes huddle together in a garden nest box for warmth, but their winter casualty rate is still high.

Candlemas forecasts

IT IS an old country saying that there is 'no trusting February weather'. And indeed always, when out walking this month, be prepared for rain was what I was taught as a boy. On balance, probably fair enough advice, but the familiar phrase 'February fill-dyke' simply cannot be substantiated.

The wettest month of the year varies according to the area and altitude at which you live. For instance, in the Vale of Belvoir a farmer neighbour who keeps records for the Severn Trent Water Authority has recorded highest monthly rainfall in most months of the year – including May, June and July – over the past twenty years.*

A day this month on which we are told to take particular not of the weather is February 2nd, Candlemas Day. This is a church festival to celebrate the purification of the Virgin Mary, and a day when – according to tradition – the weather will be determined for the rest of the year. So please take a note of a saying that has proved correct, for the most part, over a great many years:

> *If Candlemas Day be sunny and bright*
> *Winter will have another flight;*
> *But if Candlemas be cloudy with rain,*
> *Winter is gone and will not come again.*

I can assure you that although many of the handed-down weather legends do not stand up against these records, this one certainly does.

---

* In the month from mid-April to mid-May 1983 there were 28 consecutive days of rain. In 62 days from mid-March, when that wet spell began, there were only six days free from measurable rain. In my own village, out of thirteen cricket fixtures at the start of the season only two could be played.

Galanthophiles

THESE February thoughts again turn my mind to Snowdrops, part of my January radio diary but which I then admitted are more plentiful *this* month and so are called Fair Maids of February. Seeing so many more Snowdrops now out in the garden, it has dawned on me why in earlier times the festival of Candlemas and the full flowering of Snowdrops was supposed to coincide. It was then the custom to remove images of the Virgin Mary from church altars on Candlemas Day and fill the spaces so left with Snowdrops.

My passion for Snowdrops is, of course, shared by others; particularly I have in mind a number of country parsons who – rather after the manner of their leisured counterparts in the nineteenth century who were avid rosarians – collect many different species of Snowdrops, indeed saving some from extinction. Our enthusiasm gives rise to a descriptive noun: the Snowdrop lover is called a Galanthophile, from the Latin botanical word for this plant – *galanthus*. As with other plant collectors, we Galanthophiles like to give and exchange plants and it was in this way that I recently added to my small collection a Snowdrop named after the religious leader Edward Pusey (1800-82), one time Regius professor of Hebrew at Oxford. This rare variety of Snowdrop was given me by my Cambridge friend the Rev Richard Blakeway-Philips, a distinguished grower and exhibitor of alpine plants, who by chance came across a specimen of the Pusey variety somewhere in Berkshire and has since propagated it.

There are some delightful country names for Snowdrops. In Gloucestershire they call them Candlemas Bells; in Somerset it is Dingle Bells, Snowdropers or Eve's Tears; and, so very delightfully, the German for Snowdrop is *Nackte Jungfrau* – Naked Maiden.

By the middle of February I go out in search of early activity in field ponds, mainly looking for Frogs and Newts although the pity is that both have in recent years dwindled in numbers alarmingly. It is hard to find any Frog-spawn in the field ponds and this (as with the shortage of Sticklebacks I mentioned earlier) is usually put down to the poisoning effects of farm chemicals seeping into ditches and streams. Supporting this explanation is the fact that garden ponds in built-up areas away from farmland often contain plenty of Frogs – my son in East London even complains of his pool being overstocked and the same applies to my brother's Lily-covered garden pool at an old vicarage in Derbyshire (incidentally, what a pretty sight it is to see baby Frogs gazing into the world around them as they sit on a Water Lily leaf!)

In this matter of pollution it is worth noting that in the early summer of this year East Midlands' farmers were officially asked to be wary of the danger of river pollution from the disposal of silage effluent.

Valentine thoughts

A COUNTRY DIARY cannot ignore the folklore attached to St Valentine's Day on February 14th.

Here then are some useful rural tips for young ladies: if you wish to know the occupation of your future husband do take a note of the first bird you see on St Valentine's Day. A Blackbird means your husband will be a clergyman; a Robin, then a sailor; for a rich husband then it has (of course) to be a Goldfinch; a Blue Tit gets you a happy man and a Dove a good man. No bird at all – well that is dreadful; it means no man for you!

The Roman Festival of the Lupercalia, held in the middle of February, was a romantic occasion and probably the origin of St Valentine's Day. Boys would draw girls' names out of a box and be paired off accordingly for the coming year. 'Licentious games' were also part of the Festival but by the Middle Ages the church tried to make St Valentine's Day religious by having people draw saints' names out of a box and so emulate that saint in the year ahead. I have to report that by the sixteenth century girls' names were back in the boxes!

From my studious research into all this Roman and subsequent razzle-dazzle, I am also able to tell you that before 1653 Valentine greetings had to be delivered by hand – the first mailboxes in Europe appeared in Paris in that year of 1653 but they did not last long. Messengers, afraid of losing their jobs, put Mice in the collecting boxes.

Now let me add this invaluable bit of advice for the girls: put some Bay leaves under your pillow on St Valentine's night and recite:

> *St Valentine be kind to me,*
> *This night may I my true love to see.*

Gorse in bloom

Where to find the Bay leaves? Well, I really do not know in your area – but try rummaging around in any old vicarage or country doctor's shrub garden. Beneath the Walnut and Lime trees most had a Bay somewhere among the shrubbery with all those inevitable Laurels, Choisya and Garrya *elliptica*.

In the stockyard

THE first lambs on the farms can be seen from now on and somehow that always seems to stir thoughts of Spring to come, even if the wind is sharp and there are still no leaves on the trees.

At first light any morning this month literally scores of Buntings and Finches of several different kinds are busy scouring for food around the stockyard on the farm opposite the cottage. Usually two kinds of Buntings there – the Yellow Hammer and the aptly named Corn Bunting, both characterised by strong beaks needed for breaking into seeds. A pretty bird, the Yellow Hammer. I love the way he displays his vivid yellow head and breast as he sings away on the very top twigs of the hedge, a song to which country children fit the words *'A little bit of bread and no cheese-eese'*.

As for the Finches, I normally see three types feeding peacefully together, and that is something they do not do when bossing their nesting territories later on. Why do the Chaffinches, Goldfinches and Greenfinches group together in the hard weather? My guess – and it *is* only a guess – is that the habit must have some survival value connected with their feeding. In a group there are more eyes on the alert to look for food – the group finds an abundant supply at some spot, strips the patch of available seed and moves on. For a lone bird to find enough food at this time of the year would take too long. And I suppose another advantage of flocking together is the safety in numbers; birds of prey find it harder to single out one victim for attack. Incidentally, it is another good reason to get up early in the mornings just to watch Finches suddenly making a deserted landscape come alive with birds swooping up and down in a grand display of aerobatics.

Birds of a very different kind from Finches are good weather prophets, if you know what to look for in their habits. Rooks, for instance, vary the height at which they build their nests in the trees and when they build lower down rather than in the tree tops watch out for a rough Spring and Summer. Then again I expect you have noticed how Seagulls come much further inland when heavy weather is about, joining the Rooks and Lapwings in the fields.

Fairyland of lace

FEBRUARY is often a month of fog and hoar-frost, the sort of frost which produces lovely patterns of ice-crystals on our windows.

After a frost like this try and get out into the fields, or even the park, and see how every single blade of grass, every tree, shrub, hedge and twig – even delicate spider webs – are coated with crystals, making a fairyland of fern, flower and lace patterns. Very attractive, but hard weather this month can have some disastrous effects on bird life and turn their Spring timetables upside down.

While I was writing this book a friend living on the East Coast told me the sad story of nearly 800 birds being washed ashore during very rough weather in one county alone. These birds included Razorbills and Puffins. Along the Lincolnshire coastline unprecedented numbers of Arctic seabirds were blown inland, among them many Little Auks which I usually see in only very small numbers. Further north, the observatory at Souter Point near South Shields in just one day logged 4,500 Little Auks flying north trying to get back into the Atlantic. Then came a pleasant change in the weather and, a few days later, my naturalists' bush telegraph earlier referred to, brought me good news. An 'action stations' kind of call informed that a rare bird of prey called the Red Kite had been reported seen in woodlands around Belvoir – or rather, the only description I was first given was that of 'a strange large bird with a gliding sort of flight through the trees'.

My curiosity very strongly aroused I made it my business to get out in search of the mystery bird – also reported by a gamekeeper friend. No doubt about it being a Kite, and not, as I first assumed it would be, a Harrier or a Buzzard, one of which impressive birds had also been seen near Grantham at about much the same time. Seeing the Red Kite was for me very exciting since the species is officially described as having 'almost disappeared from Britain'. Years ago the Kite was a common scavenger in towns, and Lincolnshire was a nesting stronghold. A Kite seen nowadays is most probably a wanderer from the remote hills of North Wales, or perhaps from the Continent.

In February, Robins form into pairs and once a female has been accepted by the male bird he makes his voice heard quite persistently, declaring that no other Robins are to invade his chosen bit of territory. Later, the Robins favourite nesting site will be in hedge banks; rusty tin cans hidden in hedge-bottoms are another popular home and whenever I look at a nesting Robin I am delighted with the way this bird does not immediately fly off but instead sits tight, her beady eyes fixed on the intruder.

A surprise for me out in the fields at the very end of this month – a large bunch of toadstools sprouting from the trunk of an Oak around which, in the gently sloping and ridged meadow, we usually find most of our good pickings of Mushrooms back in the autumn. This Oak tree fungus is called Velvet Shanks, so named because the lower part of the stem does indeed resemble rich brown velvet. What is interesting about Velvet Shanks is that during the rest of the year the plant exists *inside* the wood of the tree trunk as a mass of branching threads called mycelium. Most other fungi stop growing as the weather gets colder, but Velvet Shanks comes into flower during the winter, so pushing out the toadstools.

There is a season and a time to every purpose under heaven. Time puts into perspective our own human hopes and disappointments, setting them against Nature's mighty and indestructible master plan – a glimpse of which I have shared with you through the twelve months which started with the coming of Spring in March.

The miracle is about to begin again.

I should like to thank BBC Radio Lincolnshire and the East Midlands Tourist Board for making this book possible; also for its attractive production in our East Midlands region. To my listeners on the radio, and my readers of this book, I also offer my sincere thanks for your company throughout *Our Country Year*, a book mainly written in the Vale of Belvoir but also partly at the great medieval Haddon Hall in Derbyshire, built between the twelfth and fifteenth centuries.

If, with this modest collection of countryside pictures in words, I have given someone pleasure – and perhaps a little new knowledge – then indeed (to quote a favourite song) 'my living shall not be in vain'.

Farewell, thou busy world, and may we never meet again:
Here can I eat, and sleep, and pray,
And do more good in one short day,
Than he who his whole age out wears
Upon the most conspicious theatres,
Where nought but vice and vanity do reign.

The Retirement
Stanzes Irreguliers to Izaak Walton, by Charles Cotton

(Publication of *Our Country Year* coincides with the 300th anniversary of the death of Izaak Walton, Stafford-born author of *The Compleat Angler*)

Greetings card from the author's Victorian family album

Terms for Groups of Wildlife

A Flight of Swallows
A Siege of Herons
A Siege of Bitterns
A Herd of Cranes
A Herd of Swans
A Herd of Curlews
A Herd of Deer
A Dropping of Sheldrakes
A Spring of Teal
A Covert of Coots
A Pudding of Ducks
A Suite of Mallards
A Nide of Pheasants
A Bevy of Quails
A Covey of Partridges
A Congregation of Plovers
A Flight of Doves
A Walk or Wisp of Snipe
A Brood of Hens
A Building of Rooks
A Mumuration of Starlings
An Exaltation of Larks

A Host of Sparrows
A Harras of Horses
A Rag of Colts
A Stud of Mares
A Pace of Asses
A Tribe of Goats
A Cete of Badgers
A Buske or Down of Hares
A Nest of Rabbits
A Drove of Cattle
A Flock of Sheep
A Pack of Hounds
A Sounder of Hogs
A Charm of Goldfinches
A Watch of Nightingales
A Brood of Grouse
A Cast of Hawks
A Desert of Lapwings
A Fall of Woodcock
A Muster of Peacocks
A Swarm of Bees, Flies
A Gaggle of Geese

A Countryman's Calendar

March

Plants   Fifty species will be found flowering in a favourable March – Wood Anemone and Lesser Celandine in woods; Blackthorn or Sloe in hedges; Coltsfoot on waste ground.

Wildlife   Chaffinch begins to sing; Thrush and Blackbird nest in hedgerows; fifty kinds of moth on the wing; Hares perform dances.

General   March 1: St David
March 14: Freshwater fishing ends
March 17: St Patrick
March 21: Vernal Equinox. First day of Spring
Normal rainfall 3.22 in
Normal sunshine 3.69 hours daily

April

Plants   Kingcups, Bluebells and Cowslips start blooming; flowers visible on Oak, Beech, Birch, Alder, Poplar and Willow.

Wildlife   Some thirty migrants arrive, including Chiff-Chaff, Willow Warbler, Sand Martin, House Martin, Whitethroat, Swallow, Nightingale, Cuckoo, Turtle Dove, Swift and Nightjar, in that order.

General April 19: Primrose Day
April 23: St George
Normal rainfall 2.52 in
Normal sunshine 5.23 hours daily

May

Plants Ash, Wild Cherry, Horse Chestnut and Mountain Ash in bloom. Many wild orchids flower in woods and chalky districts.
Wildlife Nightjar begins churring at dusk; Nightingale sings by day and night; most species nesting. Squirrels, Stoats and Weasels have young. Dawn chorus at its best in third week.
General May 2: May Day
May 29: Oak Apple Day
Normal rainfall 2.61 in
Normal sunshine 6.26 hours daily

June

Plants Honeysuckle, Dog Rose, Hawthorn in bloom. Rhododendrons at their best in woodlands.
Wildlife Nightingale and many others cease song. Cuckoo stutters; female calls with bubbling cry. Tadpoles show first legs. Hawk moths and early Dragonflies appear.
General June 21: Longest Day
June 24: Midsummer Day
Normal rainfall 2.64 in
Normal sunshine 6.36 hours daily

July

Plants Over 700 plants may be found in bloom, also grasses and sedges. Heath and Ling begin to flower.
Wildlife Little bird song, but the Yellow-Hammer sings persistently. Glow-worms lighten woodland paths at dusk. Young bats are born.
General July 15: St Swithin's Day
July 31: Gun licences expire
Normal rainfall 3.25 in
Normal sunshine 5.83 hours daily

August

Plants — Heather in full bloom; Ragwort, Tansy and Thistle in flower.
Wildlife — Swift and Swallow leave early. Butterflies and moths abundant.
General — August 12: Grouse shooting begins
Normal rainfall 3.88 in
Normal sunshine 5.34 hours daily

September

Plants — Rowan and Privet berries ripen; Blackberry abundant. Bright red spikes of Wild Arum berries in hedge bottoms.
Wildlife — Swallows and Martins congregate. Chiff-Chaff and Willow Warbler sing before they depart. Squirrels and Hedgehogs prepare for winter sleep.
General — September 1: Partridge shooting begins
September 23: Autumnal Equinox
September 29: Michaelmas Day
Normal rainfall 3.09 in
Normal sunshine 4.57 hours daily

October

Plants — Moths feast on the Ivy flowers; Autumnal tints begin, Lime and Ash leaves fall first. Mushrooms and toadstools abound.
Wildlife — Last of the summer migrants leave. Winter migrants arrive from Scandinavia – Fieldfare, Redwing and Wild Geese.
General — October 1: Pheasant shooting begins
October 2: Trout fishing ends
October 31: Salmon fishing ends
Normal rainfall 4.25 in
Normal sunshine 3.04 hours daily

November

Plants — Chickweed, Groundsel, Red Dead Nettle and Gorse still in bloom. Buds appear on the Sallow (palm).
Wildlife — Flocks of Lapwings or Peewits in the fields; Long-tailed Tits and Goldcrests in the woods.
General — November 1: Fox hunting begins
Normal rainfall 4.19 in
Normal sunshine 1.93 hours daily

December

Plants — Coltsfoot and Celandine appear in mild weather; Mistletoe berries ripe. Hazel catkins conspicuous.
Wildlife — Fresh visitors may arrive: Crossbill, Waxwing, Snow Bunting among them. Winter moths appear. Gnats dance on mild days.
General — December 10: Grouse shooting ends
December 31: Various licences expire
December 22: Shortest Day
Normal rainfall 4.72 in
Normal sunshine 1.23 hours daily

January

Plants — Snowdrop and Crocus may be in bloom, also Violet in sheltered places. Gorse, Groundsel and Dandelion in flower.
Wildlife — A few Bats out. Earthworms surface on warm nights.
General — January 1: Renew dog and other licences
January – First Monday after Epiphany – Plough Monday
Normal rainfall 3.78 in
Normal sunshine 1.47 hours daily

February

Plants — Look on Hazel twigs, where the catkins are prominent, for the tiny red flowers. Barren Strawberry and Primrose bloom.
Wildlife — Wood Pigeons coo; Rooks repair nests and begin to lay; Missel-Thrush sings from tops of trees; Frogs and Toads spawn.
General — February 1: Pheasant and Partridge shooting ends. Salmon and Trout fishing begin
February 14: St Valentine's Day
Normal rainfall 3.26 in
Normal sunshine 2.45 hours daily

From Grandma's Scrapbook

IN LATE Victorian days my paternal grandmother, born in a village on the Nottingham-Derbyshire borders, started a scrapbook of contemporary pictures, news and articles – a huge leather bound volume over two feet square and which we have in the family to this day. Not only did Grandmama record history in the making but she illustrated the scrapbook with watercolour paintings and examples of her home-made greetings cards, two of which are reproduced in my book.

Occasional dips into the scrapbook as 'tailpieces' to my broadcasts each week seem to be popular – judging by the letters I get from BBC Radio Lincolnshire listeners. Here is a small selection the household hints recorded:

> If there is snow about try making Snow Pancakes. When the batter is ready whisk into it a handful of frozen snow and your pancakes will be particularly light and crisp.
>
> When hanging a picture on the wall place a small piece of cork in each corner at the back so making a gap between the wall and the picture for ventilation. It also stops the picture frame marking the paper on the wall.
>
> To make fabrics flameproof rinse them in a solution of 2 oz of alum in a gallon of water. (Useful tip that for young children's clothes.)
>
> Use small branches of Holly, Gorse, Rose or any prickly shrub to protect garden seeds from mice and birds. Just spread the prickly branches flat over the seed drills and anchor them with some more branches placed upright.
>
> To make the leaves of house plants glossy, clean them with a sponge soaked in a little milk. Also, the leaves will not go brown if rain water rather than tap water is used. Neither should house plants be placed near fruit as this has a destructive effect on the flowers.
>
> For sore throats pour boiling water over a well-browned piece of toast, leave to infuse until cold. Strain the liquid and sweeten with honey. (It happens that I have recently been re-reading Charlotte Brontë's *Shirley* so I know where Grandma got that one from!)

If a damp room is to be re-papered, first wash the walls – after of course removing all the old paper – with a solution of half a pound of alum and a similar amount of painter's size made by dissolving these in boiling water. Wash the walls twice and re-paper when dry.

Keep a small block of beeswax in the work basket to wax thread for strong sewing. (Elsewhere in the scrapbook Grandma also wrote down for posterity that, before sewing tough things such as leather, one should always grease the needle by drawing it alongside one's nose.)

Biscuits stay crisp if a sugar lump is kept in the biscuit barrel.

Rush matting will last longer in a warm atmosphere if sprayed three times a year; and to wash cocoanut fibre doormats use hot water and soda, then rinse well with a watering can and finally brush with salt water to stiffen the fibres.

To keep cut Daffodils longer put only an inch or two of water into the vase at a time and replenish as necessary.

If you suffer from cramp at night, fill a cotton bag with old, clean corks; sew up the top and put the bag inside the end of your bed.

About the author

NOW living in an out-of-the-way Victorian cottage (a century or so ago it was a small village isolation hospital) in that rural triangle where the counties of Lincolnshire, Leicestershire and Nottinghamshire come together in the beautiful Vale of Belvoir, Dr Geoffrey Eley M.A. is back in the Midlands – his family's homeland for as long as its records go back.

To this cottage, in a small river valley just beneath Belvoir where a castle has stood for 900 years, Dr Eley has brought an abiding love and understanding of the countryside inherited in large measure from a Nottinghamshire grandmother who was one of three artist sisters specialising in landscape and botanical illustration in oils and watercolours (they also ran, in Victorian days, a private art school for 'refined young ladies'!)

Geoffrey Eley's career as writer, broadcaster and publisher has centred on Agriculture and Medicine. After wartime service as a senior officer in the BBC European Division responsible for news and aspects of psychological warfare, the author was for several years BBC Home Service agricultural talks producer at Broadcasting House in London. Later he returned to his lifelong interest in Medicine and his studies were rewarded in the 1960s by being made Editor of *Medical News*, Britain's first newspaper for doctors; being elected a Fellow of the Royal Society of Medicine; and becoming Managing Director of a medical and educational book publishing company in Cambridge and London.

In 1977 Dr Eley retired from staff appointments in favour of freelance work, mainly writing and broadcasting but also including being Adviser in Natural History to Aloha College, at Marbella in Spain. In 1981, for his long service and achievements in the illustrious 'Square Mile', the author was made a Freeman of the City of London.